FAVORITE DISHES

Bertha Honoré Palmer
Woman's Building
Chicago March 24th 1893

FAVORITE DISHES

A COLUMBIAN AUTOGRAPH SOUVENIR COOKERY BOOK

Compiled by CARRIE V. SHUMAN

Introductions by REID BADGER
AND BRUCE KRAIG

University of Illinois Press
Urbana and Chicago

Manufactured in the United States of America
♾ This book is printed on acid-free paper.

Library of Congress Cataloging-in-Publication Data

Shuman, Carrie V.
Favorite dishes : a Columbian autograph souvenir cookery book / compiled by Carrie V. Shuman ; introductions by Reid Badger and Bruce Kraig.
p. cm.
Reprint. Originally published: Chicago : R. P. Donnelley, 1893.
Includes bibliographical references.
ISBN 10: 0-252-02624-1 (cloth : alk. paper) —
ISBN 10: 0-252-06937-4 (pbk. : alk. paper)
ISBN 13: 978-0-252-02624-9 (cloth : alk. paper) —
ISBN 13: 978-0-252-06937-6 (pbk. : alk. paper)
1. Cookery, American. I. Title.
TX715.S5675 2001
641.5973—dc21 00-033794

1 2 3 4 5 C P 6 5 4 3 2

University of Illinois Press
1325 South Oak Street
Champaign, Illinois 61820-6903
www.press.uillinois.edu

CONTENTS

Fish.

Shell Fish.

Game.

Vegetables.

Eggs.

Salad.

Doughnuts and Fritters.

Cookies.

Desserts.

Ice Cream.

Candy.

Punch.

WORLD'S FAIRS AND OTHER RECIPES FOR PROGRESS

Reid Badger

A World's Fair . . . is the clearing-house of civilization.
—THOMAS W. PALMER, President,
World's Columbian Exposition

Even more important than the discovery of Columbus . . . is the fact that the General Government has just discovered woman.
—BERTHA HONORÉ PALMER, President,
Board of Lady Managers,
World's Columbian Exposition

Favorite Dishes*: *A Columbian Autograph Souvenir Cookery Book is a unique and handsome remembrance from late Victorian America and from an event that, more clearly than any other of its time, reflected the combination of energy, optimism, and uncertainty so characteristic of the era. The World's Columbian Exposition, commonly referred to as the Chicago World's Fair of 1893, or, in more culturally descriptive terms, as "The White City," was the most dramatic and extensive public display in America in the nineteenth century. Held to commemorate the four-hundredth anniversary of the European discovery of the New World, the Columbian Exposition announced the emergence of Chicago and the American West into national prominence and the entry of the United States as a major force on the world stage. If the twentieth century can reasonably be described as the "American Century," then it began in Chicago in 1893.

The World's Columbian Exposition, however, was neither the first great world's fair nor the first great fair to be held on American soil. The Great Exhibition of the Works of Industry of All Nations, the first true world's fair, was opened by Queen Victoria in London on May 1, 1851. By the time it closed five months later, more than six million surprisingly well behaved visitors had flocked to Joseph Paxton's glass-and-iron "Crystal Palace" to marvel at the more than 100,000 exhibits sent by a score of the most industrially advanced nations of Europe and the Americas. So popular and successful was this first effort that, from 1851 until the First World War, the world's fair became one of the few international institutions of Western culture. Reflecting the accelerating pace of industrial and technological innovation, commercial expansion, and increasing international competition of the period, succeeding world's fairs also gave space to displays of natural history, agriculture, education, and the arts, all of which were arranged to demonstrate progressive (as opposed to revolutionary) change and the superior evolution of Western civilization. As a consequence, participation by non-Western, indigenous, or colonial peoples, when included, was often characterized by racial stereotyping and, by today's standards at least, demeaning comparisons. Beginning at Paris in 1889, international meetings (called "congresses") were held concurrently with the fairs to provide important opportunities to address the nonmaterial, intellectual, or spiritual, aspects of human culture.

Although the world's fair originated in Western Europe, the country that produced the greatest number was the United States. Between 1853 and 1916, America hosted nineteen exhibitions that included international representation, five of which (Philadelphia in 1876, Chicago in 1893, Buffalo in 1901, St. Louis in 1904, and San Francisco in 1915) rank as major world's fairs. American interest and participation, like that of the French and the British, reflected the expansion of nationalism, competitive enterprise, and international consciousness. World's fairs in the United States, however, as with American representation in foreign fairs, depended more heavily upon private, rather than governmental, management and financial support. Since the United States lacked a clearly acknowledged representative city, the equivalent of a Paris or London, the process of selecting a suitable site in which to hold a world's fair often revealed an intensity of urban and regional rivalry not present elsewhere.

The first world's fair held in the United States was not a great success. Hastily conceived by New York businessmen to capitalize upon the success of London's great fair, the New York World's Fair of 1853 opened two months behind schedule and, in spite of newspaperman Horace Greeley's energetic promotion and showman P. T. Barnum's creative management, closed with little fanfare and a substantial debt the next year. Twenty years later, however, despite a soul-wrenching and devastating civil war, the country was better prepared.

With the one-hundredth anniversary of the Declaration of Independence approaching, hosting a great American world's fair appeared to be an appropriate way both to heal the nation's wounds and to demonstrate to the world the restoration of the American Union. Boston, Baltimore, Washington, and New York were more than interested, but Congress wisely chose Philadelphia as the centennial city, and on May 10, 1876, President Grant opened the first grand American world's fair, in Fairmount Park. Occupying 285 acres, the fair presented over 150 temporary structures erected by states, territories, and foreign governments. By the time it closed on November 10, over 8,000,000 visitors had paid to see the 30,000 exhibits representing thirty-two countries.

The focus of the Philadelphia Centennial was unquestionably the machine, the American industrial machines and dynamos being greatly admired (the 700-ton Corliss engine was the fair's most popular attraction). American exhibits in other areas, especially the fine arts, however, were not so highly regarded. As a center of national attention, the Centennial Exhibition attracted more than one hundred professional, religious, social, and reform-minded groups who chose to hold their meetings during the fair and to spread their messages to the throngs of fairgoers. In addition, in the absence of adequate federal financial backing, the officials of the Centennial Exhibition (and those of subsequent American fairs) found themselves forced to depend upon gate receipts and revenues from concessions and popular amusements. In the United States, necessarily, popular show business grew up with the world's fairs and was an important element in all of them.

Following the Philadelphia Centennial, fairs of primarily regional significance were held in the former Confederate States to demonstrate the adoption of Atlanta booster Henry W. Grady's vision of a "new" industrial South, but in 1893 the United States was to host a world's fair of much greater significance. Challenged by the impressive Exposition Universelle of 1889 in Paris, for which the Eiffel Tower was constructed, it was clear that only New York, or perhaps Chicago, possessed the private financial and physical resources required even to approach, much less surpass, the standard set by the French. The subsequent battle that was fought out in the newspaper editorials of the established eastern urban giant and its younger western challenger was one of the most bitter and vitriolic in American history, but it served to stimulate national interest in the prospective fair and to spur organizational efforts in both cities. Eventually, following a roll-call vote in the House of Representatives, the issue was decided. On April 28, 1890, President Benjamin Harrison signed a bill authorizing an international exposition to take place in Chicago during the spring and summer of 1893, rather than 1892, the more appropriate date, in order to provide an additional year for preparation.

The provisions of the legislation made it clear that doubts existed about the ability and appropriateness of Chicago to produce a major international fair that would creditably represent the entire United States. Specifically, the bill created a National Commission that duplicated one already established in Chicago to oversee and approve all major decisions relating to the choice of physical site, design of the grounds, construction of the buildings, and conduct of the exposition. This duplication of authority considerably complicated the process of producing the fair. Nevertheless, during the summer of 1890 the initial steps were taken toward deciding upon an appropriate location. Eventually, thanks to the advice of Frederick Law Olmsted, the decision was made to make Jackson Park, an unimproved 600-acre site alongside Lake Michigan and eight miles south of the city's center, the principal location of the fair. By the end of November, a basic plan had been adopted that envisioned taking advantage of the natural characteristics of the site by utilizing water as a major element in each of the two principal aspects of the physical design. The first of these, probably a result of Olmsted's influence, was a large lagoon surrounding a wooded island. The second, undoubtedly inspired by the recent French exposition, called for a grand architectural Court of Honor surrounding a formal basin, with a system of interconnecting canals and lagoons.

The responsibility for determining the architects and the architectural style for the major buildings (which would eventually hold some 65,000 exhibits) fell principally to the consulting architects, Burnham and Root, a major Chicago firm. Given the time pressures, Daniel Burnham recommended that rather than hold a competition for designs, five leading national firms (Richard Morris Hunt; McKim, Mead and White; Van Brunt and Howe; George Post; and Peabody and Stearns) should design the buildings in the Court of Honor and five Chicago firms (Adler and Sullivan; S. S. Beman; Burling and Whitehouse; Jenney and Mundie; and Henry

Ives Cobb) should be given the others. Burnham and Root chose not to design any building themselves but, in their capacity as consulting architects, elected to supervise and coordinate the overall plan. John Root was expected to play an important role in determining the overall architectural style, but during the first gathering of the architects in January 1891, he contracted a fatal case of pneumonia, and his influence on the fair was lost.

Whether Root's presence would have altered the eventual outcome is unknown, but it is true that following his death, the formal symmetrical and monumental stylistic values—those expressing imperial authority and order—gained prominence, especially in the central Court of Honor, where a more or less academic neoclassical style and color (white, thus the "White City") were decided upon. It is also true that with the loss of his partner, Daniel Burnham assumed greater responsibility and was appointed chief of construction. Burnham selected Charles Atwood, an academically trained New Yorker, to replace Root as designer in charge, and it was in this capacity that Atwood came to have a major influence on the overall architecture of the exposition, designing the formal peristyle group that closed the lake end of the Court of Honor, the Art Building (now the Museum of Science and Industry and the sole surviving structure), plus dozens of lesser buildings. Due to the influence of Augustus Saint-Gaudens, America's leading sculptor, who had been brought in as an advisor, and Frank Millet, Burnham's director of color, many of the best-known artists and sculptors in the United States were enlisted to produce the finishing decorative details. Daniel Chester French (perhaps best known now for his statue of the seated Lincoln in the memorial at Washington, D.C.) was commissioned to create the statue of the Republic for one end of the Grand Basin, and Frederick MacMonnies was chosen to provide the Columbian Fountain to balance it at the other. A greater number of American artists and architects contributed to the creation of the World's Columbian Exposition than had ever been assembled to work on a single project before, and perhaps since. Enhanced by the most extensive use of electric lighting ever attempted, the imposing and elaborate visual impression of the formal exposition buildings and grounds was undoubtedly the greatest exhibit of the Chicago World's Fair. By night, it was indeed a fairyland, and Americans were captivated by it.

But there was another fair that summer in Chicago, one whose "exuberant chaos" provided visitors with an alternative to the refined order and Beaux-Arts neoclassicism of the Court of Honor. Long before the exposition was formally announced in December 1890, scores of requests had begun pouring in from amusement vendors, restaurateurs, circus acts, musical troupes, and speculators of all sorts for space on the grounds. Fair officials had expected from the beginning to provide space for amusements and concessions because experience had shown their value in drawing crowds and providing revenue. But as the plan for the exposition developed—with its formal emphasis—what to do with the show-business element became a real question. The solution was to locate the amusement features along the narrow strip of land between Jackson and Washington Parks called the Midway Plaisance. Under the supervision of a young entrepreneur, Sol Bloom (who would, as a congressman years later, help draft the founding charter of the United Nations), the Midway at Chicago became one of the most successful and famous amusement areas of any of the world's fairs, and it established a pattern for mass entertainment that soon found application in such independent parks as Coney Island. Within the Midway were to be found German beer halls, Turkish bazaars, Egyptian jugglers, Dahomean drummers, hootchy-koochy dancers, the World's Congress of Beauty, ostrich omelets, and George Ferris's giant mechanical marvel, the ferris wheel, which carried as many as two thousand people at a time 264 feet in the air above the crowds.

When the Columbian Exposition closed on October 30, 1893, over 21.5 million paid admissions had been recorded and, despite one of the most crippling depressions of the century, a profit was returned to its investors. But the tangible results, financial or otherwise, were insignificant compared to the value of the fair as a great cultural event. To many Americans at that time, the fair was a massive demonstration of the coming of age of the United States, the cultural as well as material equal to any of the great European countries with civilizations many centuries old. Writers in search of answers to the confusing multiplicity and cutthroat competition of the modern age, such as Henry Adams or William Dean Howells, believed they glimpsed in the White City the first expressions of unity and cooperation. For Chicagoans, the fair became a landmark in the history of their city, opening up a new era of civic commitment and cultural flowering in the Midwest. The 1893 Chicago World's Fair was the most important of the American fairs of the era. Its influence was felt on all other major fairs held in the United States prior to World War I, by which time nearly every American town of any size had its own versions of the world's fair, in the forms of the department store, the supermarket, the amusement park, and that ultimate fantasyland, the movie theater. The great fair was also significant in another way, one that *Favorite Dishes* documents directly.

Among the most novel aspects of the Chicago World's Fair, and one that drew considerable attention to the enterprise in the months prior to opening, was the prospect that women were to play a conspicuous and responsible role in a world's fair for the first time. Although the first American world's fair, in New York in 1853, was an all-male enterprise, women had made an important appearance by attempting to conduct informal meetings with visitors on issues of concern to them: temperance, women's rights, and abolition. Lucy Stone, Antoinette Brown, Lucretia Mott, and Susan B. Anthony, early champions of women's interests, all came to the fair hoping to get a hearing for their messages among the throngs of people expected to attend. The crowds, however, were generally unreceptive, even sometimes insulting, and New York authorities did little to protect the women's right to speak their views in public. The *New York Herald*'s description of these advocates of equality and independence as "a gathering of unsexed women" is suggestive of the general response with which they were met.

Philadelphia's Centennial Fair of 1876 was also initially planned without considering participation by women in any fashion, but Elizabeth Cady Stanton and Susan B. Anthony, recognizing the opportunity that a world's fair presented, were so persistent in their appeals that the managers eventually agreed to permit a women's pavilion to be built on the grounds, but only on the condition that the women pay for it themselves. Benjamin Franklin's great-granddaughter, Elizabeth Gillespie of Philadelphia, took charge of both fund raising and assembling examples of the products and accomplishments of women, and a pavilion was eventually not only erected and filled with exhibits but was well received and patronized by the fair's visitors. While women's products were being treated as an interesting novelty in the woman's pavilion, women themselves were given no official responsibilities nor any governmental recognition. Their request for a place on the platform of the gala Fourth of July ceremonies was summarily refused. In response, Anthony and several other activists petitioned the fair's authorities to be allowed simply to read the Women's Declaration of Independence, which had been adopted nearly thirty years earlier at the first women's rights conference in Seneca Falls, New York. Again, the answer was no; they would be permitted neither to read their declaration nor even to present a copy of the document to the chairman of the ceremonies. Nevertheless, on the great day, Susan B. Anthony, Matilda Gage, Sara Spencer, Lily Blake, and Phoebe Couzins, after waiting respectfully for the Declaration of Independence of the United States to be read and cheered, marched through the large crowd to the platform and presented their declaration to the chairman. There was little he could do but accept it; the women marched out, distributing copies as they passed, and later read and explained their message to a friendly crowd.

In 1889, when Anthony learned that once again there was to be a great world's fair in America, she became determined that this time women's participation would be officially sanctioned and supported by the national government. She believed that if this were done it would benefit women in the United States in general and the suffrage movement, her lifelong cause, in particular. Knowing that suffrage for women was hardly popular with the national Congress, and that a number of women whose social prestige would be needed might be frightened off if suffrage were mentioned, she began quietly working behind the scenes. Contacting women in Washington whose sympathy and discretion she trusted, she encouraged them to organize meetings in their homes and invite the wives and daughters of leading Washington officials. In this discreet fashion, Anthony helped create a lobby in Congress for women to be granted a place on the fair's governing commission. When in January 1890 it was announced that a world's fair bill was being considered, she drafted a petition to that effect and obtained the signatures of over one hundred wives and daughters of congressmen, cabinet members, Supreme Court justices, and military officers.

When the act creating the world's fair was finally passed it created the usual National Commission of men to plan and supervise the enterprise, but it also authorized the appointment of an unspecified number of women to a "Board of Lady Managers." At the time, the concession was thought to be largely honorary; women were not really expected to take an active part in such a major national event and no responsibilities for the Lady Managers, or guidelines for their selection, were stipulated. Subsequently, the National Commission appointed 115 wives and daughters of prominent political and business leaders from the various states and territories to the Board of Lady Managers. At the board's meeting in Chicago on November 19, 1890, the members resolved that women's exhibits not be segregated from the main displays at the fair (as they had been at the Centennial) and that Congress would be asked for a precise definition of their responsibilities and authority, which they suggested should be more than merely advisory. At the same meeting, the women chose Bertha Honoré Palmer as their president; it was a fortunate, if somewhat obvious, selection.

From her sumptuous castle on Lake Shore Drive, Bertha Palmer, wife of Potter Palmer, a multimillionaire real-estate developer and Marshall Field's ex-partner, set the tone and dictated the cultural taste of Chicago's newly rich and influential. A member of the Fortnightly Club, the first women's literary association in the city, and an enthusiastic collector of French and American Impressionist paintings, Mrs. Palmer was also seriously concerned with public service and especially with social issues that affected Chicago's women. She was a supporter of the reformist governor John Peter Altgeld, a trustee of the new women's college at Northwestern University, and a member of the remarkable Chicago Woman's Club. Projects of the latter group included the establishment of a protective agency for women and children and an industrial school for homeless boys, and the club's support was critical to the founding of Jane Addams's Hull-House and the building of Frances Willard's Woman's Christian Temperance Union Temple. An able speaker, Mrs. Palmer was as effective in dealing with the fair's senior (male) officials as she was with various factions among the women themselves, including the major suffragist organizations, from whom she kept a safe but cordial distance.

As public attention both in the United States and abroad became increasingly focused on the novel role that women would play in the Columbian Exposition, the directors of the Chicago Company found themselves in agreement with the Lady Managers that there should be a Woman's Building erected at Jackson Park to serve as a place for exhibits and as an administrative home for the Woman's Department. In February 1891, the fair's Board of Architects further agreed that the Woman's Building should be designed by a woman architect. Twelve designs were submitted in the subsequent competition. Sophia G. Hayden of Boston (who had graduated from MIT) was awarded the contract for her Italian Renaissance design, and eventually the building was erected across the lagoon from the wooded island. At the same time, the Woman's Department contacted notable international women, women's clubs, and organizations and attempted to interest them in the fair as an agent for reforming current attitudes about woman's place in the progress of civilization. The department also created a network of boards of lady managers in the states and territories. Important women artists, including Mary Cassatt, Candace Wheeler, and Alice Rideout, were enlisted to provide decorative statuary and paintings for the building. As interest continued to rise, Mrs. Palmer and the Lady Managers found themselves deluged with requests from those wanting exhibit space or wanting to provide, as Jeanne Madeline Weimann has written in her thorough treatment of *The Fair Women* (1981), "mementoes of an emancipated era."

In a relationship not unlike that between the Court of Honor and the Midway, the Woman's Department found itself providing a salesroom in the Woman's Building that offered its patrons inexpensive commercial keepsakes ranging from bookmarks, playing cards, and postcards to commemorative silver spoons and books about the fair and the women's exhibits. Almost anyone with an idea for a souvenir that could be sold in the Woman's Building approached Mrs. Palmer for permission to sell their wares. One of the more interesting propositions came in January 1893 from Carrie V. Shuman. Shuman's proposal was to produce a cookbook, endorsed and autographed by Mrs. Palmer and the Lady Managers and containing their prize recipes. The book would then be offered to women of limited means to sell in order to pay the expenses of a visit to the fair, which they could otherwise not afford.

Mrs. Palmer, as Weimann has reported, was not enthusiastic. In her view, the commission proposed to be given the sellers was a good deal less than the cost to the publisher to produce the book and the "handling fees" to be collected by Shuman. Nevertheless, Shuman had received encouragement and several recipes from a number of Lady Managers who thought well of the idea and Mrs. Palmer felt she had little choice but to go along. When Shuman asked for a recipe from the president of the Board of Lady Managers, however, Mrs. Palmer replied that she had "not been attending to the household lately" and had none to offer. Undeterred, Shuman offered to provide a nice recipe for Roman punch to be used in Mrs. Palmer's name. Mrs. Palmer wrote back, according to Weimann, that "she would prefer the substitution of 'a simple ice or frozen pudding, as I would rather not incur the possibility of comment by endorsing a recipe for punch.' This request was ignored: the book was published with 'Mrs. Palmer's Romaine Punch' which called for one gill of sherry and two tablespoonsful of Jamaica rum." Any inclination to comment by the WCTU, or other temperance organizations, was quelled by Frances Willard, who also provided Shuman with a recipe for her book.

The actual number of copies of *Favorite Dishes* that were sold, and the number of women who thereby found means to come to Chicago to see the accomplishments of their sisters in the summer of 1893, is unknown, but it cannot have been large. Neither, in the end, were the consequences of the extraordinary effort and optimistic expectations of American women at the fair. Although the Columbian Exposition gave women more public attention than ever before and provided opportunities for them to participate more fully in an important national enterprise, it did not thereby announce a revolution. Still, *Favorite Dishes,* like the fair itself, provides a snapshot of American culture at a particularly critical time when it looked both backward and forward, at a juncture that was, in historian Henry Steele Commager's apt description, the "watershed of American history."

FAVORITE DISHES AND THE HISTORY OF AMERICAN COOKBOOKS

Bruce Kraig

I first encountered *Favorite Dishes: A Columbian Autograph Souvenir Cookery Book* several years ago while doing research on food history in the Chicago Historical Society library. On the catalog card, by its age itself a historic document, was the book's subtitle: "Over Three Hundred Autograph Recipes, and Twenty-Three Portraits, Contributed Specially By The Board of Lady Managers Of The World's Columbian Exposition." Cookery at the exposition has often been discussed and its culinary star, Sarah Tyson Rorer, the head of the Philadelphia Cooking School, published voluminously (fifty-four books alone). But few of the works on the exposition mention *Favorite Dishes.* Perhaps it was lost in the welter of souvenirs, photographs, and other memorials of this, America's first world's fair (the Woman's Building had not only its own postcards, playing cards, prints, and posters, but even silver spoons and bookmarks featuring the bust of the President of the Board of Lady Managers, Mrs. Bertha Honoré Palmer). And in later years, who might remember such Lady Managers as Mrs. Anna M. Fosdick of Alabama or Mrs. Cora L. Bartlett of New Mexico, much less their recipes? Like so many cookery books of times and culinary styles past, this one faded from memory.

Unjustly forgotten, I think. This is a marvelous book to be studied on many levels. Open the cover with its Beaux-Arts design and there is a photograph of Mrs. Palmer complete with a dated autograph. It is in her preferred style, a cameo profile, hair swept up, and a five-strand pearl necklace around her throat. She was as she looked, elegant and sure of her place in Chicago society. Scattered across the pages are portraits of other Lady Managers. They are all formal in style, most Olympian, some, like that of the Countess of Aberdeen, Romantic. Some of the women look frankly dead-on into the camera. Then there is Miss Frances E. Willard, the leading light of the Woman's Christian Temperance Union, looking sternly correct with her almost mannish hair-style and pince-nez glasses. Each recipe is autographed—with ink and nibbed pen. Some signatures are in bold hands, others delicate and small, but each is unique, like the photographs some cryptic clue to the signers' personalities. It's like finding an old photograph album or a packet of letters in the attic. We look at those faces and signatures and wonder what the women were really like, how they thought, and how they lived. Here in this volume they tell us a little about themselves, through recipes.

For us today, looking at this volume offers a glimpse into history. For contemporaries these were living, even famous, people. *Favorite Dishes* was meant to be a "celebrity" cookbook. It was less a pure cookery manual than a random collection of recipes from women who were important in their own communities and who had made this monument to "women's progress" in the arts and sciences, the Woman's Building at the White City, a success. The book has all the weaknesses of many community cookbooks, and their strengths. Recent studies show that such books have much to tell us about the lives of the (mostly) women who contributed to them.[1] But, whatever else might be deduced from the book, the recipes themselves are historical documents about cookery and foodways in the nineteenth century.

Favorite Dishes was compiled at a time when America and its foods were being transformed. Industrialization was in full swing, as was urbanization. In terms of food this meant mass production and wide distribution of products that now bore brand names. Among those at the World's

Columbian Exposition were the newly minted Cracker Jack, Cream of Wheat, Shredded Wheat, Pabst Blue Ribbon Beer, and Wrigley's Juicy Fruit Gum. Prominent, too, were Aunt Jemima (with Nancy Green playing the eponymous cook) and the H. J. Heinz Company's Sour Spiced Gherkins. It is said that a million visitors flocked to Heinz's display, where they were given small "pickle pins." Conserves and pickles were serious components of the American diet.

Foods like these were industrial products made for mass consumption. While some, such as Heinz pickles, were hand packed, foods were becoming entirely industrialized, raised with farming machinery and artificial fertilizers and cooked and packed in factories. Canned foods had long been available and, packed more safely by new techniques in the 1870s, were now widespread. The "tin" can was the symbol of a new era. Within a generation, food preparation at home would change from labor-intensive, made-from-scratch cookery to the use of "heat-and-eat" varieties of canned foods. As one observer put it, crowds of housekeepers saw in prepared foods "numberless means of increasing the health, ease, and happiness of the household with the least expenditure of time and money."[2] Flours were made by national companies such as Pillsbury and Washburn and Crosby beginning in the 1870s. These highly refined products resulted from technological innovations in milling (more efficient winnowing and steel rollers). Standardized yeasts had been introduced about the same time by companies such as Fleischmann of Cincinnati. Chicago meat producers, Armour and Swift among them, sold nationwide via the continent-spanning railroad system. By 1893 consumers in the Midwest and the Northeast could buy citrus fruits from the burgeoning Florida industry, and California was beginning to earn its reputation as the national produce center. In short, the origins of the modern food production and distribution systems lie in the late nineteenth and early twentieth centuries.

The Industrial Revolution is usually said to have had two phases: dependence first on iron and steam, then on chemistry. Two major concepts that affected food grew up in the period, especially in its later phase. One is the idea of progress through science and technology; the other, a vision of society and all of its activities as a machine. Both gave rise to specialists in all fields who sought to lead humanity forward to a better future. Understanding the underlying science in every aspect of life became important in everyday life. A whole new industry, the knowledge industry, based on science and expertise, was born. Experts taught that efficient machines are best and had much to teach people in a disordered world. Among organs of expertise were cooking schools and the field of "domestic science," later known as "home economics" and the "new nutrition."

Laura Shapiro places Catharine Beecher's *A Treatise on Domestic Economy* (1841) at the beginning of the domestic science movement, with emphasis on her chapter entitled "Habits of System and Order."[3] (*Favorite Dishes* contributor Mrs. Isabella Beecher Hooker was Catharine's half sister.) The real founder of the initiative was Ellen Richards, who in 1870 became the first woman admitted to MIT. A redoubtable scientist, she had a long career in teaching and as a consultant to industry. "Most of the domestic scientists who set the movement on its course during these decades either were trained by Ellen Richards or worked alongside her, or at the very least, owned a copy of her first book, the *Chemistry of Cooking and Cleaning*."[4] Richards's philosophy might have been summed up by the first principal of the Boston Cooking School, Mrs. D. A. Lincoln, in a speech to the World's Congress of Women at the Columbian Exposition: "'We think that it [cookery] means that many of our people have awakened to the fact that eating is something more than animal indulgence, and that cooking has a nobler purpose than the gratification of appetite and the sense of taste. Cooking has been defined as the art of preparing food for the nourishment of the human body.'"[5]

As part of the new movement, everything had to be systematized and the underlying chemistry of foods understood. W. O. Atwater, a chemistry professor at Wesleyan University, developed food composition tables in the 1890s. The principle of balanced meals based on chemical analysis of foods and their interaction with human physiology was established by this movement. Weights and measures were to be precise, as were all culinary processes. Mrs. Lincoln and her successor at the cooking school, Fannie Farmer, insisted upon exact measurements in all recipes. This required standard weights and measures, for instance, "one cup" meaning eight fluid ounces and not six, as in an ordinary teacup. Today's recipes, with their exact ingredients lists and precise instructions, to say nothing of label analysis, descend from this movement.

The new nutrition movement led to the establishment of kitchens in urban settlement houses during the 1890s. Here, menus based on scientific principles would be served to the poor, especially the many new immigrants who were pouring into the country. Economy and good nutrition were the keynotes, and the newly invented Aladdin Oven (basically a tin-lined box with a hole in the bottom for the source of its heat, a kerosene lamp) helped conscientious cooks achieve these. Reformers set up a model New England kitchen at the Columbian Exposition and served many thousands of meals cooked on Aladdins and sold for thirty-three cents each.[6] (Richards, who headed the project, had declined to appear at the Woman's Building, saying that women had progressed sufficiently so as not to warrant her appearance.) The new nutrition movement's kitchens failed by the end of the 90s, as did the oven they touted. The new breed of cooks produced dishes that were less than appetizing, especially to stubbornly traditional Jewish and Italian immigrants, and the oven was too slow and limited in its cooking abilities. There is no mention of the Aladdin in *Favorite Dishes* and the only concessions to "healthy" dishes are recipes using graham (whole wheat) flour.

The technology of cooking was changing, though not yet by much. The first fully electric stove was shown at the exposition, but it would be a full generation before this appliance gained any popularity. By the end of the century most home ovens used coal, wood, gas, or oil for fuel. Mrs. Lincoln's *Boston Cooking School Cook Book* (1884) and Fannie Farmer's more famous successor volume (1896) assumed that the cook would use a coal-fired cast-iron stove and oven.[7] Apparently so did the contributors to *Favorite Dishes.* Many cookery manuals of the time have sections devoted to the use and care of stoves. As Susan Strasser observes, these coal-fueled stoves took a lot of time to operate and maintain—an hour a day—while the cook moved 272 pounds of coal and 27 pounds of ash in a week.[8] Wood was even worse (though many dishes cooked in a wood-fired oven gain marvelous flavors). No wonder people raved about gas ovens. *The Book of the Fair* says: "A favorite resort in the Woman's Building is the model kitchen, with a floor of tiling, its gas cooking-range and modern utensils, all scrupulously clean, and in the neatest order."[9] *The New Home Cook Book,* first published in 1874, extols gas in the 1911 edition: "A well-equipped gas stove is . . . the most perfect arrangement for the presentation of food that has yet been devised." It goes on to say that in "gas regions" ordinary cook-stoves are "being converted into gas burners by simply introducing a large perforated iron pipe into the fire box."[10] The safety of these conversions is problematic, but efficiency conquers all objections.

Within a decade and a half of the Columbian Exposition, gas ovens were widespread and with them more precise control of cooking temperatures. In the older cookbooks, as in *Favorite Dishes,* oven temperatures are approximate; "slow oven," "moderate oven," and "quick oven" were the usual designations. By the 1914 edition of *Mrs. Rorer's Philadelphia Cook Book* (originally published in 1886) some of the baking and roasting instructions bore temperature markings such as 400° F for a "quick" or "hot" oven, 420° for "very quick."[11] Otherwise, cooks had to know their stoves, which dampers and flues to adjust, which part was hotter than others, and in what position to place the dish. It took some experience to know just how to cook, and all cookery manuals assumed their readers had this experience.

By the time *Favorite Dishes* appeared, kitchen equipment was on the verge of changes that allowed better control of temperatures. The assumption was that most of the stovetop cookware would be cast-iron. Most of these implements were uncoated and needed both seasoning and special care. Enameled cast-iron ware had long been available from Europe, and some had been made in the United States. In 1892 the Jacob J. Vollrath Manufacturing Company in Sheboygan, Wisconsin, began producing stamped sheet-steel utensils coated with a mottled gray-colored enamel. Speckled steel pots and pans became fixtures in American homes soon thereafter. In the same year the Pittsburgh Reduction Company (later the Aluminum Company of America, ALCOA) began producing aluminum cookware. It would be another twenty years, however, before aluminum would be widely used because it was more costly than steel. Both steel and aluminum are more temperature sensitive than cast-iron (this is the reason woks are made of these materials), so cooking techniques had to be adjusted accordingly. Frying and sauteeing, for instance, were hardly ever given precise times as they often are today. Once again, the recipe writers presumed the cook's experience. That is clearly so in most of the recipes in *Favorite Dishes* (Mrs. Helen A. Peck's "A Good Roast Turkey" and Mrs. Rufus S. Frost's marvelous "Snipe and Woodcock Broiled on Toast" being exceptions).

Favorite Dishes recipes normally assume a certain commonality in kitchen utensils. Cookery manuals often listed what equipment would be needed in a "modern" kitchen. *The New Home Cookbook* gives the following list:

Utensils
necessary in the kitchen of a small family

Wooden Ware

Kitchen Table; Wash Bench; Wash Tubs, (three sizes); Wash Board; Skirt Board; Bosom Board; Bread Board; Towel Roll; Potatoe [*sic*] Masher; Wooden Spoons; Clothes Stick; Flour Barrel Cover; Flour Sieve; Chopping Bowl; Soap Bowl; Pails; Lemon Squeezer; Clothes Wringer; Clothes Bars; Clothes Pins; Clothes Baskets; Mop; Wood Boxes (nests).

Tin Ware

One Boiler for Clothes; one Boiler for Ham; two Dish Pans; one Preserving Pan; four Milk Pans; two Quart Basins; two Pint Basins; two quart covered Tin Pails; one four quart covered Tin Pail; Sauce Pans with Covers, two sizes; two Tin Cups with handles; four Jelly Moulds, (half pint); two Pint Moulds for Rice, blanc-mange, etc.; one Skimmer; two Dippers, different sizes; two Funnels (one for Jug and one for Cruets); one quart measure, also, pint, half pint and gill measures (they should be broad and low as they are more easily kept clean); three Scoops; Bread Pans; two round Jelly Cake Pans, and two long Pie Pans; one Coffee Pot; one Tea Steeper; one Colander; one Steamer; one Horse Radish Grater; one Nutmeg Grater; one small Salt Sieve; one Hair Sieve for straining jelly; one Dover's Egg Beater; one Cake Turner; one Cake Cutter; one Apple Corer; one Potato Cutter; one Dozen Muffin Rings; one Soap Shaker; Ice Filter; Flour Dredge; Tea Canister; Coffee Canister; Cake, Bread, and Cracker, and Cheese Boxes; Crumb Tray; Dust Pans.

Iron Ware

Range; one Pot with Steamer to fit; one Soup Kettle; Preserving Kettle (porcelain); Tea Kettle; Large and Small Frying Pans; Dripping Pans; Gem Pans; Iron Spoons of different sizes; one Gridiron; one Griddle; one Waffle Iron; Toasting Rack; Meat Fork; Jagging Iron; Can Opener; Coffee Mill; Flat Irons; Hammer; Tack Hammer; Screwdriver; Ice Pick.

Stone Ware

Crocks of Various sizes; Bowls Holding six quarts, four quarts, two quarts and pint bowls; six Earthen Baking Dishes, different sizes.

Brushes

Table Brush; two Dust Brushes; two Scrub Brushes; one Blacking Brush for Stove; Shoe Brush; Hearth Brush; Brooms.[12]

Many of the same implements are found in modern kitchens, but some are specialized to nineteenth-century cooking. Clothes boilers and wringers aside, pans for milk, preserving, ham boiling, or baking gems, and the varieties of sieves, are not so common now. They were then and all cooks knew how to use them. And if this inventory reminds us of "country cooking," there is a reason—a good part of it was archaic.

Favorite Dishes: A Columbian Autograph Souvenir Cookery Book began with a proposal by Carrie V. Shuman. She suggested, in a letter to Bertha Honoré Palmer, who vetted proposals for sales at the Woman's Building, that there were women who could not afford to travel to the exposition. She expostulated: "All over the country are found mothers of families with limited means . . . who will dream longingly and hopelessly of the Exposition. While these women have not business training, yet they may be quite capable of selling books in their immediate neighborhood."[13] Mrs. Shuman estimated that the book's selling price would be $1.50, with 50¢ going to the seller. She then asked Mrs. Palmer for a recipe. At first cool to the idea because she thought that too much of the sales price was going to overhead, Mrs. Palmer relented when Mrs. Shuman received enthusiastic responses from Lady Managers across the country. The selling price may not seem exorbitant, but it was the average daily wage for a semi-skilled American worker. Admission to the fair was 50¢ for adults, 25¢ for children, with many attractions at similar extra costs. When the book was about to be printed by the Chicago firm R. R. Donnelley and Sons (who had published Chicago's first cookbook a generation before), Mrs. Palmer was again asked to donate a recipe. Being too busy for household matters, she had none. Mrs. Shuman then supplied one for her, a "Roman punch from Miss Parlor [*sic*]'s Cookbook."[14] It contained sherry and rum despite Mrs. Palmer's objections to a recipe with alcohol, to say nothing of what Frances Willard might have said. *Favorite Dishes* went through at least two printings, presumably of some five thousand each, but we do not know how many women received the intended benefits.

Shuman's introduction lauds the contributors for joining "together in this place as the exponents of the Arts of Cookery, at this stage of its best development in this country, and as cheerful assistants of women who need the encouragement and blessings of their more fortunate sisters." Noblesse oblige in cookery, perhaps, or hyperbole, there are several underlying presuppositions in this comment and in the book itself. These have to do with the nature of household arrangements among America's well-to-do, class divisions, family and local traditions, commonality of experiences among women, availability of ingredients, and, as mentioned above, cooking technology. There is also a culinary-cultural context for these recipes. They are connected to a variety of contemporary cookery manuals and the recipes were set down at a time when cooking, and writing about it, was undergoing major changes.

Favorite Dishes belongs to one of the most expansive categories of cookbooks, community or fund-raising books. Janice Longone points out that American charitable cookbooks really took off after the Civil War when moneys were needed to support widows, orphans, and wounded veterans.[15] Even earlier, in 1847, Alexis Soyer had published *Charitable Cookery, or the Poor Man's Regenerator* in London as a means of funding a soup kitchen for the city's poor.[16] Such books soon took on characteristics of other kinds of cookery publications: commercial single-author books, and promotional literature from food and cooking equipment companies. As Longone says, "Frequently recipes from cooking school publications appear in the fund-raisers, and it is likely that the cooking school cookbooks set an example, both in form and content, for America's charitable cookbooks from coast to coast."[17]

Favorite Dishes is no exception. The order of recipes is about the same as that in Mrs. Lincoln's and Fannie Farmer's Boston books. All start with breads, go to soups, fish, meats, poultry, vegetables, salads, and end with desserts. There are many desserts—more than one-third of the recipes. In common with Fannie Farmer, *Favorite Dishes* ends with recipes prepared in chafing dishes. (Mrs. Palmer often brought chafing dishes when going to dinner parties at the Prairie Avenue mansion of her friend Frances Glessner, wife of a founding partner in International Harvester.) The arrangement of recipes more or less follows the succession of dishes at a sumptuous feast and still has old European elements—salads coming during or at the end of meals.

Some recipes in *Favorite Dishes* explicitly come from other cookbooks. Popular books such as Mary Newton Henderson's *Practical Cooking and Dinner Giving* (1876–1904), Lafcadio Hearn's *La Cuisine Créole* (1885), and Mrs. Rorer's classic work are cited.[18] Others were lifted without attribution, such as Mrs. Isabella Laning Candee's "Little Pigs in Blankets" (an "amusing and appetizing dish"), which comes from Mrs. Lincoln's 1884 cookbook. Today's community cookbooks have similar characteristics, only many recipes originate in newspapers and magazines.

Why expropriate recipes from well-known sources? Several reasons come to mind. These were recipes that the correspondents thought to be the best version of dishes that were served at special meals, or were characteristic of the donors' home cookery. The recipes had been well-tested and worked. That much can be observed in Mrs. Caroline E. Dennis's "String Bean Salad," which she notes is a "French recipe," but, she says, the original dressing calls for "too much pepper for Americans" (she also sent an entirely original recipe for "Tomato Conserve"). Some, maybe all, of these *were* the best recipes that the donor had to offer. Notice Frances Willard's remark, "To tell you the truth, I never knew anything about cooking or had a particle of taste for it." But she sent her mother's "old-fashioned" recipe for doughnuts because they were so "toothsome" and a memorial to her late mother. It is also a truism that contributors to community cookbooks send not only their best recipes, but recipes that reflect well on the donors themselves. This is one reason why so many recipes in collective cookbooks are desserts (in *Favorite Dishes,* excluding cookies, 101 out of 300). As Anne Bower puts it: "Like single-authored autobiographies, community cookbooks project their authors' sense of achieved status; authors of fundraising recipe collections are mostly middle or upper middle class and proud of the social spending."[19] That being so, maybe pride in one's skills as a cook or hostess was the reason for sending the best one had to offer. Yet it was no dishonor to quote from the best authorities, such as Mrs. Rorer. After all, Mrs. Lincoln herself quotes Mrs. Henderson and the famed cookbook author and teacher Maria Parloa.

The form that the recipes take also shows continuities and says much about the audiences to whom they were addressed. *Favorite Dishes*'s recipes are small narratives, phrased as if the cook were talking directly to a reader who understands her kitchen and cookery techniques. Mrs. Edwin C. Burleigh tells us to "mix a dough nearly as you would for cream-tartar biscuits," as if she were speaking to a neighbor for whom such biscuits were second nature. There are many more like this. The narrative style is personal, representing women talking within a community of women through food. How different this is from the authoritative style of the great cooking teachers. Mrs. Lincoln had begun listing ingredients in columns, followed by precise directions, and Fannie Farmer popularized the method. Books such as *The Way to a Man's Heart,* the first Settlement House Cook Book, a collaborative fund-raising book published in 1903, has all of its recipes in the modern style.[20] The form is impersonal, perhaps "scientific" in its precision. The authors assume that the reader knows little about ingredients or techniques and so has to be taught by the recipe. This tone, of instructing strangers, is found in most cookbooks and magazine and newspaper columns today.

How many of the recipes in *Favorite Dishes* were actually prepared by the contributors is open to question, though clearly many are old family ones. Mrs. Frances Welles Shepard says of her recipe for orange cake, "I have used it for twenty-five years and know it to be excellent." But Mrs. Rufus Frost's description in her "Snipe and Woodcock Broiled on Toast" gives a hint of the extent of her involvement when she says she received guidance from a "prize cook in Washington," who is clearly African American. Did Mrs. Frost actually cook the dish, or did she direct her own cook? Mrs. Palmer and Frances Willard explicitly said that they did not spend time in the kitchen. Reading through the recipes, seeing the photographs of the well-dressed Lady Managers, and noting some well-known names among them, one suspects that most, if not all, of the contributors had household servants, including cooks. A new era of household management had arrived for some Americans. Edward Bellamy, the utopian thinker who wrote the enormously successful novel *Looking Backward,* considered contemporary kitchen work in an 1889 issue of *Good Housekeeping* magazine:

> The conviction that "no one made such pies as mother," that "no one dressed the turkey like Aunt Jane," was well founded; but mothers have long ceased to make pies and Aunt Janes are no more seen in the kitchen. The cooking of well to do private families has been given over to a succession of casual employees, of whom it may be said in defense that their cooking is quite as good as people deserve who tolerate a system which produces such cooking. . . .
>
> As a result of the revolution described, the old-time prestige of the domestic kitchen has departed and the loyalty of the American people to homemade dishes hopelessly undermined.[21]

Bellamy's solution was to institute cooperative kitchens in which professional cooks would prepare "scientifically" wholesome meals for whole communities.

Bellamy was not exaggerating, at least about the ubiquity of household help. Large numbers of young immigrant women drove down the costs of domestic labor so any family with suitable income could afford servants. America's new class system could be divided into two broad categories: those who could afford to hire servants and those who could not. Keeping servants was another matter. Writing in her journal in 1888, Mrs. Frances Glessner lamented the servant situation. "I dismissed one cook on Monday: another came to take her place, but number two dismissed this place [the] next day on account of the gas range. Number three came in on Wednesday and she walked out at once. . . . Mary the cook [is] boiling with rage because I ordered wine left from dinner poured into the cooking sherry."[22]

Complaints about the difficulty of keeping servants abound in the popular media of the period. The reason, as discussed in "The Domestic Question," in *The Chicago Housekeeping Magazine* (1889), was that many in the laboring classes would rather work in shops or factories than be servants to anyone. The forces of industrialization of the household and society as a whole were inexorable. Growing work opportunities and rising incomes in the first decades of the twentieth century turned potential house servants into householders themselves. The effect on food and food writing was dramatic, marking the difference between the recipes in *Favorite Dishes* and those directed to middle-class homemakers in *The Joy of Cooking*.

Examination of contemporary upper-class family menus, such as those of the Glessner family in Chicago, shows that many of the dishes in the fair cookbook were actually eaten by the donors no matter who cooked them. There was a commonality of food preparations across this whole stratum of American society. With some exceptions, dishes are in the English tradition with some vague French influences, the latter in cream-laced sauces (see Mrs. Wilson Patterson's "Sauce Mousseline" from "the chef of Prince Jerome Bonaparte"). The recipes also show continuity from the eighteenth century and would remain in favor well into the twentieth. For instance, a recipe for French rolls resembles those published by Eliza Smith in her *Compleat Housewife* in the mid-eighteenth century or that appear in Martha Custis Washington's collection. A South Carolina recipe for "Fricassee Chicken" is the same as Hanna Glasse's and Mary Randolph's.[23] The desserts, breads, and puddings in *Favorite Dishes* are very much in the Anglo-American tradition.

Fancy though many of the dishes may be, other recipes are down-home and some are even regional American. Cornmeal muffins, cornbreads and biscuits, Boston brown bread, apple-based dishes, fried mush, "Old Virginia Slap Jacks," and other offerings remind us of traditional American dishes. These cut across class lines because items like cornbread or biscuits were eaten by the people well down the economic and social scale. Of course, the hired cooks came from such groups. There is a democratic flavor here that seems very American.

Elements of regional food preferences appear, as one might expect. "Boston Brown Bread" and "Boston Baked Beans" appear along with "Baking Powder Biscuits." Consider these two chicken recipes printed one after the other. The first is a plain "Boiled Chicken" sent by Mrs. Edwin C. Burleigh of Maine. It calls for a skinned chicken to be fried in butter, covered with water and boiled slowly for an hour, seasoned (presumably with salt and pepper), and served with thickened gravy. The next recipe, from Miss Katharine L. Minor of Louisiana, is "Jambolaya (A Spanish Creole Dish)." Mrs. William Reed from Maryland provided a recipe for "Wild Duck in Maryland." Here ducks are roasted without stuffing, well browned on the outside although "the blood should run when cut with a knife." The flesh is to be served with fried hominy and fresh celery, though currant jelly will also do. A few regional recipes would not have been familiar to all readers. Recipes sent in by delegates from New

Mexico are for enchiladas and tamales, although Señora Don Manuel Chaves's tamale recipe—given in Spanish—does not tell the reader how to make them. Tamaleros, tamale sellers, actually sold them at the fair and on Chicago's streets, but more than likely these products were made with cornmeal grits, nothing like the originals.

Whatever else it might be—a collective cookbook, a social document—*Favorite Dishes* is about what upper- and middle-class Americans ate in the nineteenth century. Consider oysters. Mrs. Shuman has a separate page in which she says that "Blue Points [East Coast] are the only proper oysters to serve for luncheon or dinner." Oysters were ubiquitous in that century's cuisine, across the country. While certainly eaten today, their presence in the midwestern heartland is largely relegated to dressings for Thanksgiving and Christmas turkeys. Then, under "Shellfish," appear terrapin recipes, four of them. The instructions are not pleasant to contemplate—bleeding, decapitation, boiling the creatures alive—but terrapins were commonly eaten at the time. Like turtle soup today, terrapin was an expensive dish for which chicken was substituted in "Mock Terrapin" recipes.[24]

Nineteenth-century cuisine was notoriously heavy in meat. Here, of the two hundred or so recipes excluding desserts, thirty-eight are for meats, fifty-nine including fish and shellfish. Among these, sweetbreads are notable. Few home cooks today prepare calves' thymus or pancreatic glands, but then they were expected parts of fancy meals. As for vegetables and grains, there are seventeen recipes that include potatoes, beans, macaroni, or rice. The only cruciferous vegetable is cauliflower (with tartar sauce); the only other "greens" appear in "Stuffed Green Peppers" and "Beets." Obviously, ordinary people ate green vegetables, especially in the South, but those were apparently too pedestrian for a celebrity cookbook. Only nice composed salads that show the cook's art would do.

Vegetables and salads are outdone in numbers alone by puddings. No category shows the British origins of the American diet more than puddings. Medieval and early modern in origin, here they are elaborated in solid, steamed forms and many softer, baked ones. Bread and chocolate puddings, perhaps some Indian puddings, are probably all that remain of this tradition, though some people still make and eat plum and Christmas puddings in the appropriate season. Suet puddings have virtually all disappeared. That is not the case with doughnuts and fritters, cakes, cookies, and desserts. Most of the cakes here are British, but several have deeper American roots. Election cakes, such as Mrs. Helen C. Brayton's and Mrs. Virginia T. Smith's, descend from early nineteenth-century editions of Amelia Simmons's *American Cookery* (1796).[25] Charlotte Russe was immensely popular, as the four recipes for it in *Favorite Dishes* demonstrate. It was invented by the great chef Antoine Carême early in the century and remained on menus until the 1970s. One recipe that never made it into standard cookbooks was Señora Don Manuel Chaves's recipe for "Tamales de Dulce." The recipe calls for soaking the correct kind of white corn and grinding it on a grinding stone into a wet paste called "nis[x]tamal," then beating, stuffing, wrapping, and steaming the delectable tamale. No Anglo reader, much less German or of other European ethnicity, would have made it because it is authentically Mexican. Here, though, in the midst of historic recipes, is a portent of future cookery in North America—ethnic foods and foodways entering the mainstream.

For those who want to try some of the recipes in *Favorite Dishes,* I urge you to do so. They mostly work, even if some of the ingredients in the recipes have been omitted. Many dishes would make the modern dietary reformers blanch, but they are very good to eat. And making one of these dishes brings to mind a time past; it is history lived—and assimilated.

Notes

Special thanks to culinary historians Susan Ridgeway and James Dano for sharing their original research on the Glessner family's culinary history. Thanks also to Joe Carlin of Food Heritage Press for finding several long-out-of-print cookery books used by the Lady Managers and other valuable information.

1. See, for example, Anne L. Bower, ed., *Recipes for Reading: Community Cookbooks, Stories, Histories* (Amherst: University of Massachusetts Press, 1997).

2. Alice Freeman Palmer, quoted in Jeanne Madeleine Weimann, *The Fair Women* (Chicago: Academy, 1981

3. Catharine Beecher, *Miss Beecher's Domestic Receipt Book* (New York: Harper, 1846).

4. Laura Shapiro, *Perfection Salad: Women and Cooking at the Turn of the Century* (New York: Farrar, Straus and Giroux, 1986), p. 40.

5. Ibid., p. 71.

6. Harvey Levenstein, *Revolution at the Table* (New York: Oxford University Press, 1899), p. 58.

7. See Mrs. D. A. Lincoln, *Boston Cooking School Cook Book* (1884; rpt. Mineola, N.Y.: Dover, 1996); Fannie Merritt Farmer, *Original 1896 Boston Cooking School Cook Book* (Mineola, N.Y.: Dover, 1997).

8. Susan Strasser, *Never Done: A History of American Housework* (New York: Pantheon, 1982), p. 41.

9. Hubert Howe Bancroft, *The Book of the Fair* (Chicago: Bancroft Company, 1893), p. 286.

10. *The New Home Cook Book, Compiled from Recipes Contributed by Ladies of Chicago and Other Cities and Towns* (1874; rpt. Chicago: McClurg, 1911), p. 25.

11. Mrs. S. T. Rorer, *Mrs. Rorer's Philadelphia Cook Book: A Manual of Home Economics* (1886; rpt. Philadelphia: Arnold, 1914).

12. *New Home Cook Book,* pp. 56–57.

13. Weimann, *Fair Women,* p. 469.

14. Ibid., p. 471.

15. Janice Bluestone Longone, "'Tried Receipts': An Overview of

America's Charitable Cookbooks," in Bower, *Recipes for Reading,* p. 20.

16. Alexis Soyer, *Charitable Cookery, or the Poor Man's Regenerator* (London, 1847).

17. Longone, "'Tried Receipts,'" p. 18.

18. See Mary Newton Henderson, *Practical Cooking and Dinner Giving: A Treatise Containing Practical Instructions in Cooking, in the Combination and Serving of Dishes, and in the Fashionable Modes of Entertaining at Breakfast, Lunch, and Dinner* (New York: Harper, 1877); Lafcadio Hearn, *La Cuisine Créole* (New York, 1885).

19. Anne Bower, "Bound Together: Recipes, Lives, Stories, and Readings," in *Recipes for Reading,* p. 31.

20. Mrs. Simon Kander and Mrs. Henry Schoenfeld, *The Way to a Man's Heart* [*The Settlement Cook Book*] (1903; facsimile edition, Bedford, Mass.: Applewood Books, 1996).

21. Edward Bellamy, "A Vital Domestic Problem, Household Service Reformed," *Good Housekeeping,* Dec. 21, 1889, p. 76.

22. "Glessner Household Journal," Glessner House Museum Archive, Chicago, Ill.

23. Hanna Glasse, *The Art of Cookery Made Plain and Easy . . . ,* 7th ed. (London, 1760); Eliza Smith, *The Compleat Housewife; or, Accomplish'd Gentlewoman's Companion,* 5th ed. (Williamsburg, Va., 1742); Mary Randolph, *The Virginia Housewife: or, The Methodical Cook* (Washington, D.C., 1824).

24. Farmer, *Original Boston Cooking School,* p. 233.

25. Amelia Simmons, *American Cookery* (1796; rpt., Grand Rapids, Mich.: William B. Eerdmans, 1965).

FAVORITE DISHES

FAVORITE DISHES

A COLUMBIAN AUTOGRAPH SOUVENIR COOKERY BOOK

OVER THREE HUNDRED AUTOGRAPH RECIPES, AND TWENTY-THREE PORTRAITS, CONTRIBUTED SPECIALLY BY THE BOARD OF LADY MANAGERS OF THE WORLD'S COLUMBIAN EXPOSITION

Illustrated by....
MAY ROOT-KERN
MELLIE INGELS JULIAN
LOUIS BRAUNHOLD
GEORGE WHARTON EDWARDS

COMPILED BY
CARRIE V. SHUMAN, CHICAGO
1893

Favorite Dishes *is due to the fact that the noble women who have labored for the best interests of mankind and womankind, in the development of the Women's Department of the World's Columbian Exposition, found time to contribute this collection of recipes, as a means of enabling the compiler to open an additional avenue for women to provide the necessary funds to pay the expenses of a visit to the Exposition.*

The compiler is most happy to congratulate the Lady Managers and Lady Alternates of every State and Territory of the United States, including Alaska, upon the fact that their prompt responses to the statement of the object of this publication bring them together in this place as the exponents of the Art of Cookery, at this stage of its best development in this country, and as cheerful assistants of women who need the encouragement and blessings of their more fortunate sisters.

It is to be regretted that all of the letters of commendation cannot be published, but as they would alone constitute a fair sized volume, only a few have been inserted.

TEA

TASTES differ as to which of the many kinds of tea is the best, and yet the general use of English Breakfast and Oolong warrants the recommending of these two teas as standard. The Chinese have taught us the correct idea of tea drinking ; to have it always freshly made, with the water boiling, and to steep the leaves at table.

The tea table can be easily equipped now with a boiler in silver or brass, with alcohol lamp underneath ; a tea caddy in china or silver, with teapot and cups before the hostess.

No set formula can be prescribed for quantity to each cup, but it averages one-half teaspoon of tea leaves.

Heat teapot by pouring in some hot water, let it stand a few moments and empty in a bowl for hot water on the table. Place tea leaves required in the pot, pour in boiling water, instantly replace the lid and let it steep a few minutes. It is then ready to serve. Use a small amount of sugar and no cream, as both cream and sugar detract from the correct flavor of tea.

For "Five O'clock Tea" a "teaball" is recommended. The teaball is convenient at all times, but especially upon an occasion when guests are coming and going. Keep the water on tea table constantly boiling and the teaball partly filled with tea leaves. A cup of tea can then be brewed quickly by dropping the ball into the cup, pouring boiling water over it, holding it in the cup (slightly moving the teaball around through the water), until the color is satisfactory to the drinker's taste. In this way three or four cups of tea can be served quickly and the flavor of the tea leaves preserved. If agreeable to the taste, a slice of lemon can be added to each cup and a few drops of arrack to make tea *á la Russe*.

Chocolate

To MAKE good Chocolate is not easy. One's own taste must be the guide regarding strength. Soften and smooth the chocolate with cold water in a jar on the range; pour in boiling water, then add milk, stirring constantly. Serve as soon as it boils. When each cup is filled with the chocolate, place two tablespoons of whipped cream on top.

Cocoa

Cocoa has the same flavor as chocolate, but it is richer and more oily.

When made from the ground it can be prepared at the table, but it is better boiled a short time in water and thinned with hot milk.

Made from the shells it requires a longer boiling. First wet two ounces of the cocoa shells with a little cold water and pour over them one quart of boiling water. Boil for one hour and a half; strain and add one quart of milk, also a few drops of the essence of vanilla.

When it comes to a boil take immediately from the fire and serve.

Coffee

THE standard mixture of coffee is Java and Mocha; two-thirds Java and one-third Mocha, the former giving the strength, the latter the flavor. After roasting it should

be kept in an air-tight can. Grind only so much each time as may be required. To one cupful of ground coffee add one beaten egg and four tablespoons of cold water; mix thoroughly in coffee pot and pour in one quart of boiling water. Stir the coffee until it boils, then place it on the back of the stove where it will simmer for ten minutes. Add a dash of cold water; wait a moment, then pour off carefully into silver coffee pot, which has been standing with hot water in it.

Filippini's recipe for Black Coffee is as follows: "Take six scant tablespoonfuls of coffee beans and grind them in a mill. Have a well cleaned French coffee pot; put the coffee on the filter, with the small strainer over, then pour on a pint and a half of boiling water, little by little, recollecting at the same time that too much care cannot be taken to have the water boiling thoroughly. When all the water is consumed, put on the cover and let it infuse slightly, but on no account must it boil. Serve in six after-dinner cups. Coffee should never be prepared more than five minutes before the time to serve."

MRS. VIRGINIA C. MEREDITH

Steamed Brown Bread.

(A LA OAKLAND FARM.)

From MRS. VIRGINIA C. MEREDITH, of Indiana, Vice Chairman Executive Committee, and Lady Manager.

It gives me great pleasure to send you an excellent recipe for steamed brown bread for your Columbian Autograph Cook Book.

I have great sympathy with your plan, and sincerely hope that the ladies of our Board will respond cheerfully to your requests.

Very sincerely,

Virginia C. Meredith

One cupful of sweet milk; one cupful of sour milk; two cupfuls of corn meal; one cupful of wheat flour; one-half cupful of New Orleans molasses; one teaspoonful of soda. Steam three hours.

Light Bread.

From MRS. GOVERNOR JAMES P. EAGLE, of Arkansas, President of State Board and Lady Manager.

Take one teacup of *boiling water;* stir in corn meal to make a stiff mush; let stand over night in moderately warm place. Then take one cup of *fresh milk* and one of warm water and heat together to a simmer and add to this the prepared mush, one tablespoonful of sugar and one teaspoonful of salt. To these ingredients add a little flour at a time, until you make a stiff batter. Place all in a milk-warm vessel of water, place near fire and keep warm until it rises—about six hours. To this yeast add flour to make a stiff dough, using one tablespoon of lard and a little salt. Keep warm till it rises and bake about an hour and a half.

Franklin Gems.

From Mrs. L. M. N. Stevens, of Maine, Lady Manager.

Mix one-half pint of milk and one-half pint water, into which stir Franklin flour until about as thick as pancakes. Pour into a very hot, well buttered gem pan and bake in a quick oven.

Baking Powder Biscuit.

From Mrs. Rollin A. Edgerton, of Arkansas, Secretary of State Board, and Lady Manager.

To one quart of flour add two teaspoons of baking powder, one more of salt, and a tablespoon of lard; mix with sweet milk sufficient to roll out on board without sticking; cut with biscuit tin and bake quickly in hot oven.

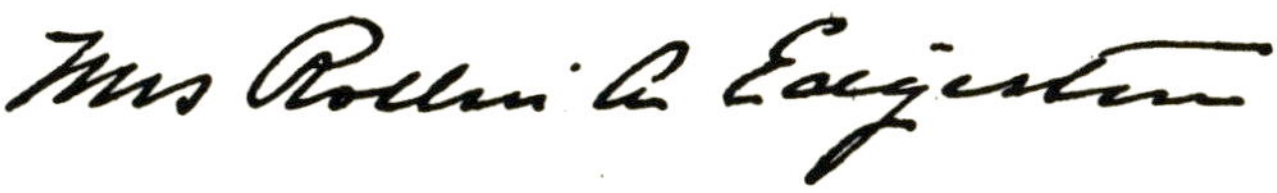

French Rolls.

From Mrs. Sallie Howard Bush, of Alabama, Alternate Lady Manager

One and one-half lbs. of flour; four oz. of butter; one-half teacup of sweet milk; one-half cake of yeast; one teaspoonful of salt; four eggs beaten very light and added last. Set to rise and bake as other rolls.

Risen Muffins.

One quart of flour; one pint of sweet milk; one cake of yeast; three eggs; one tablespoonful of butter and one of sugar; one teaspoonful of salt. The yeast must be dissolved in a little of the milk. If desired for breakfast, they must be made the night before; if for tea, set them to rise about 11 o'clock in the morning. When well risen, put them in the tin muffin rings that come especially for them and place in a moderately warm position, letting them stand about an hour before putting in to bake.

Breakfast Rolls.

From Miss Meta Telfair McLaws, of Georgia, Alternate Lady Manager.

Take one-half cake of best yeast and dissolve in half a cup of tepid water. Pour this on some sifted flour—about half a pint in quantity—to which must be added more tepid water (or milk, if you like) until a thick batter is produced. Add to this batter a pinch of salt and a little sugar. Cover well with a thick cloth and set in a warm place to rise. In the morning add lard and enough flour to make a stiff dough. Now make into roll shape and arrange them in a tin pan. Set the rolls under the stove or near it until they rise again, before putting them in the oven to bake. Rolls should be made of best flour and the batter should be put in some earthen vessel when set to rise.

Meta Telfair McLaws

Pocket-Book Rolls.

From Mrs. Ida M. Ball, of Delaware, Lady Manager.

One pint milk; one-half pint boiling water; salt and flour enough to make a sponge; one-half cake of compressed yeast. Rise for about two hours. Then add the white of one egg (beaten); mixed butter and lard the size of an egg; one teaspoonful sugar. Stiffen with flour; make out into thick sheets of dough; cut out with a circular cutter; fold one edge of the biscuit, so cut, toward the center, putting a small piece of butter under the overlapping edge of dough. Put biscuit in pans to rise, and when light, bake in a quick oven.

Potato Rolls.

From MRS. THEO. F. ARMSTRONG, of Delaware, Alternate Lady Manager.

One and one-half teacup of mashed white potatoes; one-half teacup of melted lard; one and one-half teaspoon of salt; one teacup of yeast; two eggs; one tablespoon of sugar. This is the sponge. Set to rise about nine o'clock in the morning; when light, put in enough flour to make a soft dough; then let it rise again; when light, roll out thick and cut in round cakes; put in pan and lighten again; bake in quick oven.

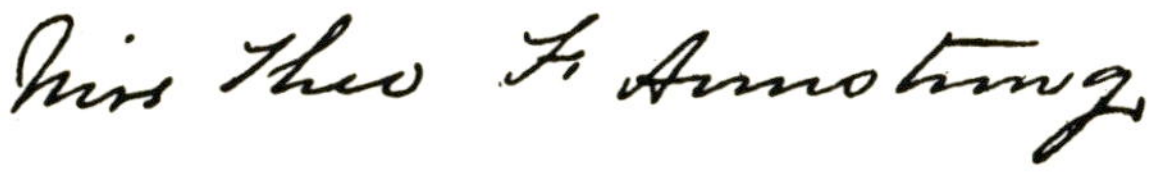

Graham Gems.

From MRS. LOUISE CAMPBELL, of New Mexico, Alternate Lady Manager.

Four cups graham flour; one tablespoon of sugar; pinch of salt; one teaspoon of soda, which dissolve in buttermilk; mix with buttermilk into a stiff batter; put into hot gem irons and bake in a quick oven.

Corn Cake.

From Miss Hattie T. Hundley, of Alabama, Lady Manager.

One pint of milk; half a pint of Indian meal; four eggs; a scant tablespoonful of butter; salt; and one teaspoonful of sugar. Pour the milk boiling on the sifted meal. When cold, add the butter (melted), the salt, the sugar, the yolks of the eggs, and, lastly, the whites, well beaten. Bake half an hour in a hot oven. It is very nice baked in iron or tin gem pans, the cups an inch and a half deep.—*Mrs. Henderson's Cook Book.*

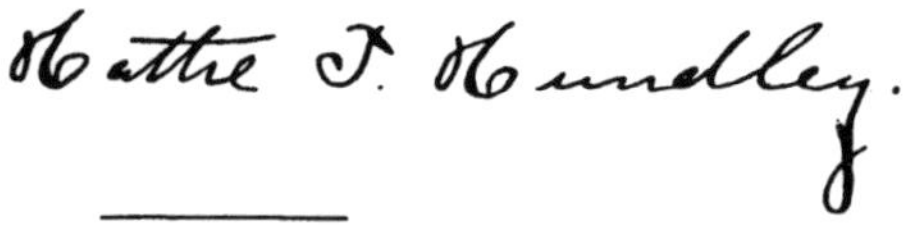

Bachelors' Corn Pone.

From Mrs. Mary B. P. Black, of West Virginia, Alternate Lady Manager.

One pint sifted corn meal; one pint buttermilk (or other sour milk or cream); two eggs, beaten separately; tablespoonful of butter and lard (half and half); little salt, and scant teaspoonful baking soda. Pour the buttermilk into the sifted corn meal, stirring until smooth, retaining a small quantity (half teacupful) of buttermilk to dissolve soda; add yolks of eggs, well beaten; then soda, having dissolved the same in the retained buttermilk, mixing well, while it effervesces; then lard and butter, either melted or cut into shreds; lastly, white of eggs, beaten to stiff froth. Bake in shallow pan, 20 or 25 minutes.

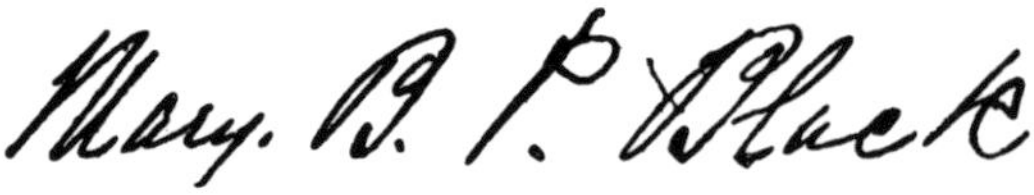

Corn Bread.

From MRS. T. J. BUTLER, of Arizona, Lady Manager.

One cup of corn meal; one half cup of sugar; one cup of sweet milk; one and one-half spoonfuls baking powder; flour enough to make a stiff batter. Bake in a quick oven.

Mrs. T. J. Butler.

Corn Meal Muffins.

From MRS. PARTHENIA P. RUE, of California, Lady Manager.

One teacupful of corn meal; one and one-half teacupfuls of flour; two teaspoonfuls yeast powder; two tablespoonfuls sugar; one tablespoonful of butter; one and one-half teacupfuls of milk; one egg or two yolks of eggs.

Parthenia P. Rue.

Baked Corn Bread.

From MRS. MINNA G. HOOKER, of VERMONT, Alternate Lady Manager.

One teacup cream; one-quarter teaspoon soda; one cup flour; butter size of a walnut; one cup sugar; one cup Indian meal; one egg. Granulated meal is the best.

Minna G. Hooker.

Steamed Brown Bread.

From MRS. E. V. MCCONNELL, of North Dakota, Lady Manager.

Two cups corn meal; one cup flour; two cups sweet milk; one cup sour milk; two-thirds cup molasses; two teaspoons (even) soda; one tablespoon salt. Steam constantly for three hours.

E. V. McConnell

Raised Brown Bread.

From MRS. ELLEN M. CHANDLER, of Vermont, Lady Manager.

Three pints corn meal; two pints shorts, or coarse flour; three-quarters cup yeast; one and one-half cups molasses; one and one-eighth quarts warm water. Let rise until it cracks on top. Steam six hours and bake slowly one hour. If wheat shorts cannot be procured, use one pint rye and one and one-half pints graham flour.

Ellen M. Chandler

Boston Brown Bread.

From MRS. GOVERNOR JAMES P. EAGLE, of Arkansas, President of State Board, and Lady Manager.

One pint of bread sponge; one cup of warm water; three-fourths cup of molasses, in which is stirred one-half teaspoon of soda: one large teaspoonful of salt. Stir in

MRS. JAMES P. EAGLE.

sufficient quantity of graham flour to make a stiff batter, put in mould and let rise till quite light and then bake in moderate oven one hour.

Mrs. James P. Eagle

Strawberry Short Cake.

From Mrs. Governor Edwin C. Burleigh, of Maine, Second Vice President, Board of Lady Managers.

Mix a dough nearly as you would for cream-tartar biscuits, only put considerable shortening in. Roll thin; bake in a pan; when done, split it and put the berries (mashed in sugar) between. Whipped cream over the top makes it very nice.

Mrs. Edwin C. Burleigh

Strawberry Short Cake.

From Mrs. Augusta Truman, of California, Alternate Lady Manager-at-Large.

Hull and rinse one quart of perfectly ripe berries; put in a bowl with one large cup of granulated sugar; cut—do not mash—with a silver spoon and set away in the ice-box for two hours. Make a rich biscuit dough, adding double quantity of butter; roll out one inch thick and bake in a deep pie-plate. When done, split quickly with a silver knife, using the knife as little as possible; spread the berries on the lower section and cover with the upper; sift on some fine sugar and serve immediately, as this recipe is for hot short cake.

Augusta Truman.

Orange Short Cake.

From Mrs. M. D. Owings, of Washington, Lady Manager.

Orange shortcake is very nice. The only difficulty to overcome in making this toothsome dish is to get rid of the white fibers which intersect the pulp of the orange, and this is, after all, a very easy matter. To prepare the oranges, simply cut them in half, without peeling, and take out the lobes precisely as when eating an orange with a spoon. The shortcake is made like very short, soft biscuit and baked in a round tin in a quick oven. When it is done, split it, sprinkle sugar over the prepared oranges, put a layer on the under crust, replace the upper part, upon which put more of the prepared oranges and serve at once with cream.

M. D. Owings

Sally Lunn.

From Mrs. Margaret M. Ratcliffe, of Arkansas, Alternate Lady Manager.

One pint of milk; three eggs, well beaten; salt; one large spoon of butter; half a teacup of yeast, and as much flour as will make a thick batter. Pour into a cake pan and place in a warm spot to rise. Bake in moderate oven. When done, cut with sharp knife crosswise twice, pouring over each part drawn butter. Replacing the parts, cut then like cake, serving at once while hot. This is a great favorite with Southerners.

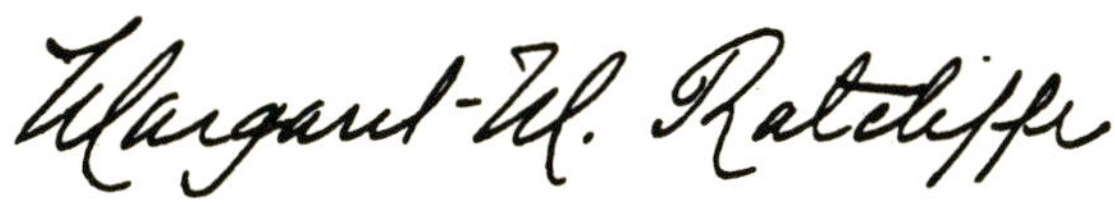

Ham Toast.

From Mrs. Rosine Ryan, of Texas, Lady Manager-at-Large.

Your enterprise commends itself to every woman who has the best interests of her sex uppermost in her thoughts.

Among the happy recollections of my childhood, luncheon Ham Toast stands out temptingly clear. It was my mother's own, and I give it in preference to several others that occur to me. Most cordially yours,

Boil a quarter of a pound of *lean* ham; chop it very fine; beat into it the yolks of three eggs, half an ounce of butter and two tablespoonfuls of cream; add a little cayenne; stir it briskly over the fire until it thickens; spread on hot toast; garnish with curled parsley.

Oat Meal.

From Mrs. George Hoxworth, of Arizona, Alternate Lady Manager.

Dampen the meal, put it in a thin cloth and steam for thirty minutes. Keeps its flavor much better than when boiled.

Brewis.

From Mrs. Frances E. Hale, of Wyoming, Lady Manager.

Take half a loaf of Boston brown bread; break in small pieces; put in an oatmeal kettle and cover with milk; boil to a smooth paste, about the consistency of oatmeal. Eat hot, with sugar and cream. Nice breakfast dish.

Frances E. Hale

Sandwich Dressing.

From Mrs. Mariam D. Cooper, of Montana, Alternate Lady Manager.

Mix two tablespoons mustard with enough hot water to make smooth; three tablespoons olive oil; very little red or white pepper; salt; yolk of one egg; mix with hand and set aside to cool; warm to spread.

Mrs Mariam D Cooper

Oysters

Blue Points are the only proper oysters to serve for luncheon or dinner. They should always be served in the deep shell, and if possible upon "oyster plates," but may be neatly served upon cracked ice, covered with a small napkin, in soup plates. The condiments are salt, pepper, cayenne, Tabasco sauce, and horse radish. A quarter of lemon is also properly served with each plate, but the gourmet prefers salt, pepper, and horse radish, as the acid of lemon does violence to the delicious flavor of the freshly-opened bivalve. Clams should be served in precisely the same way.

Bouillon

Bouillon is made of beef, and must be rich and nutritious. Take ten pounds of good clear beef cut from the middle part of the round. Wipe and cut the meat into pieces. Put this into one gallon of water and heat slowly; skim just as the water begins to boil. When this is done place the pot where it will simmer slowly for five or six hours. One hour before removing add two blades of celery, ten pepper corns, six cloves, small stick of cinnamon, and salt. Should one prefer it plain, do not put in the spices. Strain and cool. Before using, take off all fat. It is then ready to heat and serve in cups for luncheons and teas.

Soup

THE foundation of all excellent soup is a stock made from beef. For a dinner company heavy soup is not so desirable as a good, clear, rich soup, and I add a tried recipe from "Practical Cooking and Dinner Giving," called:

Amber Soup.

"A large soup bone (two pounds); a chicken; a small slice of ham; a soup bunch (or an onion, two sprigs of parsley, half a small carrot, half a small parsnip, half a stick of celery); three cloves; pepper; salt; a gallon of cold water; whites and shells of two eggs, and caramel for coloring. Let the beef, chicken and ham boil slowly for five hours, add the vegetables and cloves, to cook the last hour, having fried the onion in a little hot fat and then in it stuck the cloves. Strain the soup into an earthen bowl and let it remain over night. Next day remove the cake of fat on top; take out the jelly, avoid the settlings and mix into it the beaten whites of the eggs with the shells. Boil quickly for half a minute; then, removing the kettle, skim off care-carefully all the scum and whites of the eggs from the top, not stirring the soup itself. Pass through a jelly bag, when it should be very clear. Reheat just before serving, and add then a tablespoonful of caramel to give a rich color and flavor.

Caramel—Take a cup of sugar and a tablespoon of water. Put in a porcelain kettle and stir constantly to prevent burning, until it has a bright brown color. Then add a cup of water, pinch of salt; let it boil a few moments longer, cool, strain, and put away in a close-corked bottle—and it is always ready for coloring the soup.

Carrie V. Shuman

Mock-Turtle Soup.

From Mrs. BERIAH WILKINS, of District of Columbia, Fifth Vice President, Board of Lady Managers.

This soup should be prepared the day before it is to be served up. One calf's head, well cleaned and washed. Lay the head in the bottom of a large pot. One onion; six cloves; ten allspice; one bunch parsley; one carrot; salt to taste; cover with four quarts of water. Boil three hours, or until the flesh will slip easily from the bones; take out the head; chop the meat and tongue very fine; set aside the brains; remove the soup from the fire; strain carefully and set away until the next day. An hour before dinner take off all fat and set on as much of the stock to warm as you need. When it boils drop in a few squares of the meat you have reserved, as well as the force balls. To prepare these, rub the yolk of three hard boiled eggs to a paste in a wooden bowl, adding gradually the brains to moisten them; also a little butter; mix with these two eggs, beaten light; flour your hands; make this paste into small balls; drop them into the soup a few minutes before removing from the fire. A tablespoonful of browned flour and brown sugar for coloring; rub smooth with the same amount of butter; let it boil up well; finish the seasoning by the addition of a glass of sherry. Serve with sliced lemon.

Mrs Beriah Wilkins.

Julienne Soup.

From MRS. SUSAN R. ASHLEY, of Colorado, Sixth Vice President, Board of Lady Managers.

The day before needed, put two pounds of beef cut from the lower part of the round, into two quarts of cold water and let come slowly to the boil, skimming carefully until perfectly clear. When this point is reached, add a small onion, two stalks of celery, two cloves, and keep at the boiling point for seven hours; then strain into an earthen bowl and let cool until next day. A half hour before needed, skim off all the fat, add pepper and salt to taste; also a half pint of mixed vegetables which have been cooked in salted water and cut in uniform dice shape. Let come to a boil, and serve.

Susan R. Ashley.

Noodle Soup.

From MRS. FRONA EUNICE WAIT, of California, Alternate Lady Manager.

To make a good stock for noodle soup, take a small shank of beef, one of mutton, and another of veal; have the bones cracked and boil them together for twenty-four hours. Put with them two good sized potatoes, a carrot, a turnip, an onion, and some celery. Salt and pepper to taste. If liked, a bit of bay leaf may be added. When thoroughly well done, strain through a colander and set aside until required for use. For the noodles, use one egg for an ordinary family, and more in proportion to quantity required. Break the eggs into the flour, add a little salt, and mix into a rather stiff dough. Roll very thin and cut into fine bits. Let them dry for two hours, then drop them into the boiling stock about ten minutes before serving.

Corn Soup.

From Mrs. M. D. Thatcher, of Colorado, Lady Manager.

One large fowl, or four pounds of veal (the knuckle or neck will do). Put over fire in one gallon of cold water, without salt. Cover tightly and simmer slowly, until the meat will slip from the bones, not allowing it to boil all the strength out, as the meat can be made into a nice dish for breakfast or luncheon, by reserving a cupful of the liquor to put with it in a mince on toast, or a stew. Strain the soup to remove all bones and bits of meat. Grate one dozen ears of green corn, scraping cobs to remove the heart of the kernel (or one can, if prepared corn be used). Add corn to soup, with salt, pepper and a little parsley, and simmer slowly half an hour. Just before serving, add a tablespoonful of flour, beaten very thoroughly with a tablespoon of butter. Serve very hot.

Celery Soup.

From MRS. ALICE B. CASTLEMAN, of Kentucky, Alternate Lady Manager.

Put a veal bone to boil in one quart of water. After skimming it well, put in one pint of celery cut up very fine, two tablespoonfuls of rice, one onion, one teaspoonful of celery salt. Let this boil till reduced to a pint. Take out the meat and pass the soup through a colander, mashing and extracting as much of the puree as possible, passing the stock through it two or three times. Boil a quart of milk separately; rub two tablespoonfuls of flour in a half a cup of butter; add this to the boiled milk; after cooking it a few minutes, add the milk to the celerv puree and serve at once, mixing milk and puree well.

Oyster Soup.

From MRS. HELEN C. BRAYTON, of South Carolina, Vice President of State Board, and Lady Manager.

Take one hundred oysters and simmer in their liquor with allspice. As the scum rises skim carefully. Strain off the liquor and add to it three-quarters lb. butter and one-quarter lb. flour, rubbed to a cream. Let this boil and carefully stir in a quart of milk, guarding against curdling and pour over the oysters.

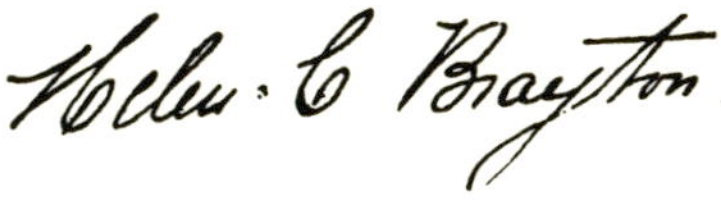

Bisque of Crab or Crawfish.

From Mrs. Belle H. Perkins, of Louisiana, President of State Board, Lady Manager.

Boil one dozen crabs; pick them in flaky pieces as much as possible; remove the meat from the claws and the fat from the back. Reserve some of the nicest pieces and put them aside for the soup after it is done. Boil a chicken or veal bone; put it into two quarts of cold water; let it come to a boil and skim well, adding a cup of rice; let all boil together until the ingredients are reduced to one quart; add an onion, a piece of celery (or a teaspoon of celery salt); pass the stock and rice, together with the other parts of the crab, through a sieve; mash the chicken or veal bone well and add some of the stock. Mash again and scrape from the bottom of the sieve, obtaining all the puree possible; add this to the broth, together with the meat of the crabs. Let a pint of sweet cream come to a boil, adding it to the soup just as it is being served; also two tablespoons of butter, celery salt and pepper.

Belle H. Perkins

Potato Puree.

From Mrs. James R. Deane, of California, Lady Manager.

Two pounds potatoes; two ounces butter; two tablespoonfuls chopped onions; two tablespoonfuls chopped celery; one quart milk; one quart boiling water; one-half cupful sago; one-half teaspoonful pepper; one teaspoonful salt. Wash, peel and slice potatoes, onions and celery. Melt the butter and add it to the vegetables, stirring it for five

MRS. FRANCIS B. CLARKE.

minutes to keep it from browning or burning. Then add the boiling water. When the vegetables are soft, rub them through a sieve; add the milk, and when the soup is boiling, add the sago, a little at a time, and cook until the sago looks clear. Stir the soup well and add seasoning the last.

Mrs. James R. Deane

Asparagus Soup.

From Mrs. Laura P. Coleman, of Colorado, Lady Manager.

Two quarts veal stock; two bunches asparagus; two cloves; two onions; three pepper corns; a little parsley. Boil one hour and strain, then add one pint whipped cream. After dished, season with salt to taste. Tapioca or celery may be substituted for asparagus.

Laura P. Coleman

Tomato Soup.

From Mrs. Ida M. Ball, of Delaware, Lady Manager.

One quart of canned tomatoes; one quart of boiling water; one small onion; one carrot; celery and parsley; one teaspoonful salt. Boil slowly for three hours and strain. Add two tablespoonfuls sugar, one tablespoonful butter, two tablespoonfuls flour made into a paste with water and used as thickening.

Ida M. Ball.

Tomato Soup.

From Mrs. E. J. P. Howes, of Michigan, Lady Manager.

Take one-half dozen fresh tomatoes or a pint of canned, and stew a half hour in a pint of water; strain through a colander; put the liquid on the fire; stir in a teaspoonful of soda; then add a pint of heated milk; season with a little butter (a dessertspoonful); salt and pepper to taste, and bring the whole to a boiling heat and serve hot.

Gumbo Filé.

From Mrs. Anna M. Fosdick, of Alabama, Lady Manager.

Cut up a chicken; sprinkle with flour, and fry in the vessel in which the gumbo is to be made. When the chicken is nearly done, chop an onion and fry with it. Pour on this three quarts of boiling water, and let all boil slowly till the flesh leaves the bones of the chicken. Then add the liquor from the oysters, two tablespoonfuls of tomato catchup, and salt and pepper to taste. Let this boil a short time; then add one hundred oysters. Do not allow them to boil more than two minutes. Remove the vessel from the fire, and before pouring into the tureen, sprinkle in two tablespoonfuls of filé. Serve always with rice.

To Prepare Filé for Gumbo.—Gather sassafras leaves, as late as possible in the season, before they turn red. Dry them in the shade and open air. When perfectly dry, pound them, sift the powder and bottle it. Keep tightly corked.

Gumbo Soup.

From MRS. VIRGINIA T. SMITH, of Connecticut, Alternate Lady Manager.

Fry three rather thin slices of salted pork; and three large onions in the same fat. Fry also a chicken of medium size, after which put pork, onions, chicken and a half pound of *lean* ham, into a dinner kettle containing four quarts of boiling water. When the mixture begins to boil, add one quart of gumbo, the corn cut from two ears, three tomatoes, and two VERY small red peppers. Add boiling water as it needs and cook slowly five or six hours, after which strain and serve with bread "crunchers" cut in dice.

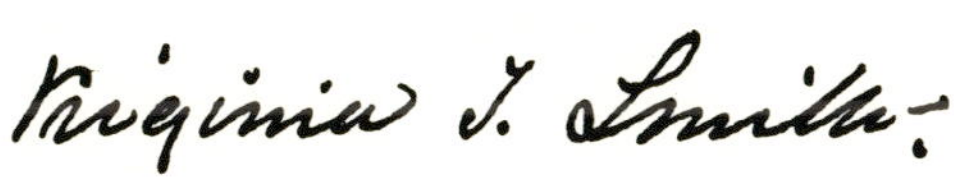

Chicken Gumbo with Oysters.

From MRS. ALICE B. CASTLEMAN, of Kentucky, Alternate Lady Manager.

Take a young chicken or a half grown one; cut up; roll it in salt, pepper and flour, and fry it a nice brown, using lard or drippings as if for a fricassee. Cut up a quart of fresh green okra and take out the chicken and fry the okra in the same lard. When well browned, return the chicken to the pot and boil. Add to it a large slice of ham — a quarter of a pound will be about right for this gumbo. Pour on to the chicken, ham and okra half a gallon of boiling water and let it boil down to three pints. Ten minutes before serving, pour into the boiling soup two dozen fine oysters, with half a pint of their liquor; let it come to a good boil and serve with well-boiled rice.—*La Cuisine Creole.*

Okra Soup.

From MISS FLORIDE CUNINGHAM, of South Carolina, Lady Manager.

Two quarts of okra cut very fine in three quarts of water, in which put a large shank of beef, and boil one hour. Then skim well and add two quarts of fresh tomatoes, strained. Boil slowly and without ceasing for at least five hours. Season with salt to the taste when the tomatoes are put in, and add black and cayenne pepper when ready to serve. Keep closely covered while cooking.

Black Bean Soup.

From MRS. M. D. FOLEY, of Nevada, Lady Manager.

Soak one coffee cup black turtle beans over night in cold water. Add water enough in the morning to cook thoroughly. One hour before dinner rub through a sieve and stir in three pints plain beef stock. Season with salt, pepper, and a salt spoon each of cloves and allspice. Just before serving add a wine glass of port or sherry, one small lemon thinly sliced and one hard boiled egg chopped fine.

Bean Soup.

From Mrs. Anne B. Patrick, of Colorado, Alternate Lady Manager.

Take one can of Boston baked beans. Remove all the pork and pour over the beans one quart of boiling water, and let it boil slowly for one hour, adding hot water from time to time to keep up the quantity. Mash the beans thoroughly and strain through a sieve, heat again nearly to boiling and add one pint of hot (not boiling) cream; add pepper and salt to taste.

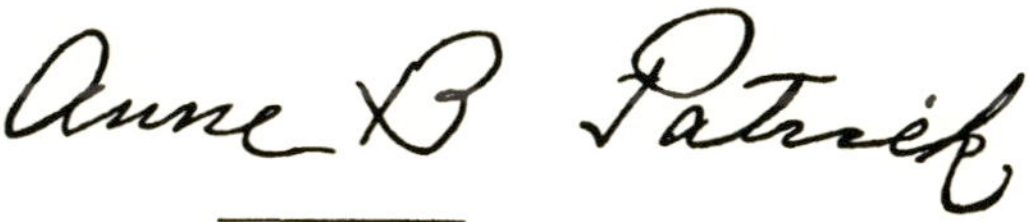

Soup Regency.

From Mrs. Isabella Beecher Hooker, of Connecticut, Lady Manager.

The bones and remains of cold fowls, such as turkey and chicken: or game, such as partridges, woodcock, etc.; two carrots; two small onions; one head of celery; one turnip; one-half tea cup pearl barley; the yolks of three eggs, boiled hard; one-quarter pint of cream; salt to taste, and two quarts of common stock.

Mode—Place the bones and remains of the fowls in the stew pan, with the vegetables sliced; pour over the stock and simmer for two hours; skim off all the fat and strain it. Wash the barley and boil it in two waters before adding it to the soup; finish simmering in the soup, and when the barley is done take out half and pound the other half with the yolks of the eggs. When well pounded, rub it through a fine colander, add the cream and the salt, if necessary; let it boil up once more and serve very hot, putting in the barley that was taken out first. Time of cooking, 2½ hours. Seasonable from September to March. Sufficient for eight persons.

Isabella Beecher Hooker

Pea Soup.

From Mrs. Whiting S. Clark, of Iowa, Lady Manager.

Cover a quart of green peas and a very small onion with hot water; boil till soft enough to strain through a sieve. Cream two tablespoons of butter and one of flour and add to a quart of milk and coffee cup of cream. Boil all together and strain. Stir in whipped cream and serve with buttered toast cut in small squares.

Mrs. Whiting S. Clark

Clam Chowder.

From Mrs. Charles H. Olmstead, of Georgia, Lady Manager.

To one pint of clams add one quart of milk, two onions, chopped fine, two tablespoonfuls of butter, the yolks of two eggs rubbed in two tablespoonfuls of flour, salt, parsley, cayenne pepper, half teaspoonful allspice, four hard-boiled eggs sliced, and half pint sherry wine added when served. Cut the soft part of the clams in two pieces; mince the tough part very fine and boil it one hour in a quart of water before adding the soft part; after the soft part has boiled half an hour longer, add the milk, flour and other ingredients. Serve hot.

Mrs Charles H Olmstead

Clam Chowder.

From Miss Lida M. Russell, of Nevada, Lady Manager.

Two large onions, sliced and fried with one cup of finely chopped salt pork. Add to it three pints of boiling milk and juice of one can of clams, in which has been cooked two large potatoes, thinly sliced; a pinch of red pepper; salt; two tablespoonfuls of flour, rubbed smooth with one tablespoon of melted butter. Stir in clams, heat well and serve at once.

Lida M Russell

Soles or Smelts Cooked with Maître D'Hotel Sauce.

From Mrs. James R. Deane, of California, Lady Manager.

Skin the fish and cut flesh into filets; put the skin and bones into a saucepan with water enough to cover them; let this boil to make the stock for the gravy. Now wipe the filets dry and roll them up with the skin side inward to make them stand firm; place the filets on a buttered baking tin, first rolling them into bread crumbs. When ready to cook, squeeze over each filet about a teaspoonful lemon juice and put on each a piece of Maître d'Hotel butter; cover with a buttered paper and cook about ten minutes.

To Make Maître d'Hotel Butter—Work one tablespoonful of butter to a cream; squeeze in the juice of one-half a lemon; one-quarter saltspoonful cayenne; one tablespoonful finely chopped parsley. Put butter on ice to cool before using.

Sauce for this Dish—Two tablespoonfuls of butter, melted; two tablespoonfuls of flour, stirred into the butter and cook for ten minutes. Then put in a small pinch of cayenne pepper and a cupful of fish stock and cook for ten minutes. Then put in juice of one-half lemon, a tablespoonful of finely chopped parsley, and just before serving put in two tablespoonfuls of cream.

Mrs. James R. Deane

Baked Shad.

From MRS. MARY R. KINDER, of Delaware, Lady Manager.

Make a stuffing of bread crumbs, butter, salt, pepper, and an egg well beaten. Stuff the shad, sew it up and bake in a quick oven. Serve with *brown gravy*, mushroom, or tomato ketchup.

Cubion.

From MRS. ANNA M. FOSDICK, of Alabama, Lady Manager.

Cut a red-fish or red-snapper in pieces and fry brown. While frying the fish, in a separate vessel, cut very fine and fry, one onion and two cloves of garlic. When brown, add two tablespoonfuls of flour, one pint of prepared tomatoes, pepper and salt to taste, a tablespoonful of Worcestershire sauce, and half a dozen whole cloves. Let this simmer for one-half hour, then add one-half pint of wine. Pour over the fried fish, and serve immediately.

Cod Fish Balls.

From MRS. A. M. PALMER, of New York, Alternate Lady Manager.

One pound codfish; one and a half pound potatoes; one-quarter pound butter; two eggs. Boil the fish slowly, then pound with a potato masher until *very* fine; add the potatoes mashed and hot; next add butter and one-half cup milk and the two eggs. Mix thoroughly, form into balls, and fry in hot fat.

Mrs A. M. Palmer

Salmon Croquettes.

From Mrs. George W. Lamar, of Georgia, Alternate Lady Manager.

One can of salmon, minced very fine; two large Irish potatoes, boiled and mashed; half of a small onion, chopped fine; two raw eggs; salt and black pepper; two tablespoonfuls of Worcestershire sauce. Rub these together until very light. Make into balls, roll in cracker dust and fry in boiling lard.

Mrs George W. Lamar

Shell Fish

Maryland Terrapins.

From Mrs. William Reed, of Maryland, Lady Manager.

After bleeding them an hour, put them into warm water. A young one will boil tender in half an hour. They are done when the shell is easily removed. Be careful not to cut off the heads before boiling, as it will make them watery. In picking them, be careful not to break the gall or waste the liquor. The small bones are often left in the terrapin—if they are Diamondbacks. Be careful not to break the eggs. When picked, add the liquor, and to three medium sized terrapins, three-fourths pound of butter, salt and pepper (cayenne) to taste. Let them stew for a short time, but be careful not to stir them more than is absolutely necessary. If you wish, one-half pint of good wine can be added just before serving.

Another way to dress terrapin is to add to the liquor of three terrapins, three-fourths pound of butter thickened with browned flour, cayenne pepper and salt. Spices or onions are never used in Maryland to dress terrapins.

Mrs William Reed

Terrapin White Stew.

From Mrs. James R. Deane, of California, Lady Manager.

Two large terrapin; three tablespoonfuls butter; one pint cream; one-half pint sherry or Madeira; one gill water; six hard-boiled eggs; one-half a lemon; two level teaspoonfuls salt; cayenne, white pepper, mace and allspice to taste. Cut up the terrapin fine; put in a stew pan with terrapin juice, water, butter, salt, pepper and spices. Simmer for fifteen minutes. Mash yolks of eggs well and mix gradually with cream; add this mixture, with the wine, and the lemon cut in thin slices, to the terrapin stew. Cut up the whites of eggs in thin rings and, stirring, mix thoroughly, but do not let it boil. To be served at once.

Mrs. James R. Deane

White Stew of Terrapin.

From Mrs. George W. Lamar, of Georgia, Alternate Lady Manager.

Cut off the heads and throw into cold water for about an hour to draw the blood. Scald them to loosen the skin and nails; open and clean them. Cover with water and boil, with part of an onion chopped fine, and a sprig of parsley and thyme. When thoroughly done, remove all the meat from the shells and bones, chop fine and return to the pot. Rub to a cream one-quarter pound of butter and one tablespoonful of flour, with a little of the stock, and stir in gradually, adding salt and red pepper to taste. Just before serving put in one-half pint of cream and one wineglass of wine to each terrapin. Slice one lemon and four hard-boiled eggs into a tureen, pour the stew over them and serve in terrapin dishes.

Terrapin Croquettes.

From Mrs. W. W. Kimball, of Chicago, Lady Manager.

Take the meat of one terrapin. Chop in small pieces, add a pint of sherry and boil ten minutes; then add a quart of cream and boil again ten minutes; add salt, cayenne pepper, a little Worcestershire sauce and two tablespoons of cream sauce. Beat up yolks of four eggs in some cream butter and mix with the other. Put in tin moulds and place on ice for six or eight hours until hard. Dip moulds in hot water to loosen. Take out of moulds, bread as you would oysters, and fry.

Deviled Lobster.

From Mrs. Joseph C. Straughan, of Idaho, Lady Manager.

Two lobsters, each weighing about two and a half lbs.; one pint of cream; two tablespoonfuls of butter; two of flour; one of mustard; a speck of cayenne; salt; pepper; a scant pint of bread crumbs. Open the lobster and with a sharp knife cut the meat rather fine. Be careful in opening not to break the body or tail shells. Wash these shells and wipe dry. Join them in the form of a boat, that they may hold the prepared meat. Put the cream on to boil. Mix the butter, flour, mustard, and pepper together and add three spoonfuls of the boiling cream. Stir all into the remaining cream and cook two minutes. Add the lobster, salt and pepper, and boil one minute. Fill the shells with the mixture and place in pan. Cover with the bread crumbs and brown for twenty minutes in a hot oven. Serve on a long narrow dish, the body in the centre, the tails at either end. Garnish with parsley.

Lobster Croquettes.

From Mrs. Louise L. Barton, of Idaho, Alternate Lady Manager.

One pint chopped lobsters; good half pint rolled crackers; one tablespoonful butter; ten of milk; salt and pepper to taste. This quantity is enough for twelve persons.

Deviled Crabs.

From Mrs. Cora L. Bartlett, of New Mexico, Lady Manager.

Take butter the size of an egg; melt slowly in saucepan; into butter slice fine a piece of onion size of a filbert; brown slowly. Sift into above, tablespoonful of flour and

MRS. EDWARD L. BARTLETT.

cream carefully; heat a generous half pint of milk and stir into butter and flour. Take No. 2 can of deviled crabs; strain off all the liquor; season with a scant teaspoon of mustard, scant teaspoon cayenne pepper, half teaspoon salt, good half teaspoon of liquor from Crosse & Blackwell's chow-chow, one teaspoon Worcestershire sauce, tablespoonful vinegar and a half teaspoon lemon juice; parsley to taste. Mix *thoroughly*, and stir into butter and milk. When cooking well, stir into it rapidly two eggs that have been well beaten. Remove from stove and put in crab shells with butter the size of filbert and rolled crackers on top. Heat in quick oven and serve at once, garnished with parsley.

This recipe makes an amount sufficient for eight persons. If desired, cracker crumbs very fine may be added to increase the quantity, just before stirring in the eggs. The crabs may be kept three or four days if in a cool place.

Cora L Bartlett

Deviled Crabs.

From Mrs. Anna E. M. Farnum, of Idaho, Lady Manager.

Boil them, take the meat out of the bodies, and large claws; put it into stew pan with half a pint of claret, spoonful of eschalot vinegar, a little cayenne, some salt, piece of butter. Stew for an hour over a gentle fire until they are almost dry. Then add small quantity of fish stock, or gravy, a tablespoonful of essence of anchovy, and small piece of butter rolled in flour. Serve with sippets of fried bread around the dish.

Anna E. M. Farnum

Deviled Crabs.

From MISS JENNIE TORREYSON, of Nevada, Alternate Lady Manager.

Have one large crab picked from the shell, and shred fine, and the shell well cleansed. Beat one egg well, add one *tea*-cup sweet cream; butter, size of an egg, melted; one sherry glass of sherry; one large spoonful of Worcestershire sauce; mace, allspice and cloves to taste; a good deal of cayenne and a little black pepper and salt. Stir this all together over the fire till it boils; then pour over the crab and mix well; fill the shell and sprinkle over the top a thick layer of fine cracker crumbs and bits of butter. Put in a hot oven till browned on tcp. Serve hot.

Jennie Torreyson

Soft Shell Crabs.

From MRS. GEORGE W. LAMAR, of Georgia, Alternate Lady Manager.

Plunge the crabs into boiling water and leave for about ten minutes. Wash them carefully and remove the sand bags. Dry them thoroughly and for one dozen crabs have six raw eggs, well beaten. Dip each crab into the eggs and roll them in cracker dust seasoned with salt and black pepper. Fry a light brown, in boiling butter or lard.

Mrs George W. Lamar

Frog Legs.

From Mrs. Ella Ray Miller, of Idaho, Alternate Lady Manager.

Frog legs must be first salted and then dipped in a batter made of cracker dust and beaten eggs. Fry them in sweet table butter until they are a golden brown color. The batter retains their sweet juices and they need no other condiments.

Pannée Oysters.

From Mrs. Alice B. Castleman, of Kentucky, Alternate Lady Manager.

Drain two dozen or more oysters in a colander. Pour over them draining from them, one quart of ice water. Put an iron skillet or frying pan on the fire; let it get almost red hot. Then put in the oysters, shaking and stirring them until they boil; add a little salt and pepper, one large tablespoonful butter. The dish must be hot and the oysters must be served *very* hot; must not stand a minute. Soda crackers put in the stove to get hot and brown, and the oysters poured over them, are very nice.

Creamed Oysters.

From Mrs. Mira B. F. Ladd, of New Hampshire, Lady Manager.

Parboil one pint of oysters in their own liquor until they are plump. Drain thoroughly and have your cracker crumbs and white sauce ready. Put a layer of oysters on a platter, then the white sauce over them, and a layer of the crumbs on top. Bake about twenty minutes or until they are brown. For this quantity of oysters use a cup of cracker or bread crumbs and about one-third of a cup of butter, melted and stirred into the crumbs. To make the white sauce, take two tablespoonfuls of butter, one pint of milk, two heaping tablespoonfuls of flour, one-half teaspoonful of salt and one-half saltspoonful of pepper. Heat the milk. Put the butter in a granite saucepan and when it bubbles stir in the dry flour very quickly until well mixed. Pour on one-third of the milk, let it boil up and thicken, then add slowly the rest of the milk. It should be free from lumps before you put in the last of the milk. Let it boil a little, then add the pepper and salt; also a tablespoonful of lemon juice and a little celery salt.

Mrs. B. F. Ladd.

"Little Pigs in Blankets."

From Mrs. Isabella Laning Candee, of Illinois, Alternate Lady Manager.

This amusing and appetizing dish is easily made. Take large fine oysters and drain them well, and season with salt and pepper, and a drop of lemon juice if desired. Cut fat bacon into very thin, even slices, and wrap each oyster in a slice of bacon, fastening securely with a wooden skewer—a toothpick will do. Two cloves can be inserted at one end of the roll to simulate *ears*. Have the frying pan very hot, and cook the little pigs until the bacon crisps. Serve immediately upon small pieces of toast.

Escalloped Oysters.

From Miss Meta Telfair McLaws, of Georgia, Alternate Lady Manager.

Spread cracker crumbs on bottom of baking dish; then place bits of butter and a layer of oysters, which must be sprinkled with salt and pepper. Make alternate layers of oysters, cracker crumbs, salt, pepper, and butter until dish is full. Have crumbs on top. Now make a small incision in center and pour in one well beaten egg, with a small quantity of oyster liquor. Put in hot oven and brown nicely.

Creamed Shrimps.

From Mrs. M. D. Foley, of Nevada, Lady Manager.

Cover one can of shrimps with cold milk and allow to come to a boil; then drain. Rub one tablespoonful flour with same quantity of butter and add slowly one cup rich milk or cream at the boiling point. Season with salt, pepper, and nutmeg, and enough tomato juice to color a shrimp pink. Stir in the shrimps and when hot pour over small squares of toast arranged on a warm platter. Garnish with sliced lemons.

Mrs. M. D. Foley.

LUNCHEON TABLE.

SAUCES

Sauce Mousseline.

From MRS. WILSON PATTERSON, of Maryland, Alternate Lady Manager.

I am always interested, and do my best to help anything done to help other women.

I send you a recipe which I hope may be of service to you. It is a delicious sauce for asparagus and is given me by the chef of Prince Jerome Bonaparte.

Wishing you every success in your most worthy undertaking, I am,

Sincerely yours,

Put in a sauce pan a piece of butter, melt it, add a pinch of flour; work it together thoroughly, wet it with a little warm water, salt it, make it boil, add the yolk of an egg; then beat up the sauce with a little fresh butter; pass it through the finest gauze. At the minute of serving add two spoonfuls of beaten cream, well mixed.

Boiled Egg Sauce.

From MRS. JAMES R. DOOLITTLE, JR., of Chicago, Lady Manager.

One large tablespoonful butter; two small tablespoonfuls flour; two eggs. Put the butter in a tin pan over boiling water; when melted, stir in flour. When thoroughly and smoothly mixed, add enough milk to make it the proper consistency for sauce. Boil the eggs hard, cut them in small pieces, stir them into the sauce, and serve with fish or boiled mutton.

Mrs. James R. Doolittle Jr.

MEATS

Filet of Beef.

From Mrs. Governor Oglesby, of Illinois, Lady Manager.

Filets of beef may be supplied by the butcher already trimmed and larded, but a more economical way is to buy the large piece which contains the tenderloin. Have the butcher cut the tenderloin out and the rest of the meat into slices one-half or one inch thick; these pieces may be used to advantage in beef olives, stews or pies, the bones in the piece of meat to be broken up for the soup pot. The filet is then to be prepared by the cook in this manner: Remove all skin and fat; fold the thin end under and skewer in place; the upper side must present a smooth surface for larding; with a larding needle lard the filet of beef in regular and even rows, with strips of firm, fat pickled pork one-quarter of an inch square and about two and one-quarter inches long. The lardoon should be about one-third of an inch under the surface and come out about three-quarters of an inch from where it went in, one-half inch projecting on each side. Place the filet in a small baking pan, with minced salt pork and suet on the bottom of the pan, and six spoonfuls of stock to baste the filet. One-half to three-quarters of an hour will roast it, depending on heat of oven and whether it is preferred underdone or well done. Serve with mushroom sauce or à la jardinière.

Mushroom Sauce—Melt one tablespoon butter; stir in a tablespoon of flour, and when it is well browned, add, after heating, six tablespoons of stock with half the juice from the can of mushrooms and one-half teaspoonful of lemon juice, seasoned with pepper and salt; add the button mushrooms and let all simmer about ten minutes. Pour over the filet of beef and serve.

À la Jardinière—Potatoes, turnips, beets, and carrots, cut in round balls, tiny onions, cauliflower blossoms, French beans or peas, are boiled separately in salted water, seasoned with salt, butter and cream, drained and then piled in little groups around the filet of beef, each pile being one kind of vegetable.

Beef Olives—Slices of beef one-half inch thick and about four inches square, spread with a force meat of cold meat, bacon or ham, with one cup of bread crumbs, the yolks of three eggs, one pint of gravy or stock, a tablespoon of catsup, salt and pepper to taste. Roll up the slices of beef and fasten with tiny skewers; brush them over with egg and crumb and brown slightly in the oven; then put in stew pan and stew till tender. Serve in gravy in which they were cooked, with fried or toasted croûtons of bread.

Roast Beef.

From Mrs. Matilda B. Carse, of Chicago, Lady Manager.

In roasting meats of all kinds, the method adopted should be the one that in the most perfect manner preserves

MRS. MATILDA B. CARSE.

the juices inside the meat. To roast beef in the best possible manner, place the clean-cut side of the meat upon a *very* hot pan. Press it close to the pan until seared and browned. Reverse and sear and brown the other side. Then put at once in the oven, the heat of which should be firm and steady, but not too intense, and allow 20 minutes to the pound; if it is to be rare, less half an hour deducted from the aggregate time on account of searing. For example, a five-lb. roast of beef will require one and one-quarter hours, a six-lb. roast one and one-half hours, and so on. If the oven is not too hot, the beef requires no basting. When it is at the proper temperature and the cooking is going on all right, the meat will keep up a gentle sputtering in the pan. A roast of beef should never be washed but carefully wiped off with a damp cloth. When meat is done, take from the oven, cut off the outside slices, then salt and pepper well. The meat, if roasted in this way, will be sweet, juicy and tender.

Yorkshire Pudding.

From MRS. HARRIET A. LUCAS, of Pennsylvania, Lady Manager.

This pudding, as its name indicates, is a great English dish, and to be used as vegetables are, with *roast beef only*. When vegetables are scarce, it adds a change to the ménu, which everybody likes, but few know how to make successfully, because *it is so very simple.*

For a small family, put one pint of milk into a bowl, a small pinch of salt; break into this (without beating) two fresh eggs. Now have a good egg beater in your hand; dust into this one-half pint of sifted flour; beat vigorously and rub out all the lumps of flour. Have ready a smaller roasting pan than that in which your beef is roasting, and put in it a good tablespoonful of sweet lard, *very hot;* pour your light batter into this, place a spit or wire frame in the pudding, lift the roast from the pan about 20 minutes before it is done and put it on the spit, so that the juices of the beef will drop on to the pudding. About 20 minutes will cook it. Make gravy in the pan from which the roast has been removed. Slide into a hot meat dish and serve with the meat. Most cooks persistently raise it by adding some sort of baking powder, thinking it of no importance that the meat is over the pudding.

I never yet found a person that did not enjoy a *good* Yorkshire pudding. This is a small one, for four or five persons. If you increase the pudding, also select a larger pan, as the batter should be fully one-half to an inch in the pan· if not, it will become too crusty.

Roulards.

From Mrs. Ralph Trautmann, of New York City, First Vice President Board of Lady Managers.

Secure slices of beef cut very thin from the round or cross rib. Take tomatoes, carrots, onions, celery, parsley, and hard boiled eggs, all chopped very fine. Mix with a good sized piece of butter, cracker crumbs, a pinch of ginger and salt and pepper to taste. Mix well and spread on the slices of beef. Make a roll of each slice, folding in the edges to retain the dressing, and tie up securely with cord. Have beef suet on the fire; after rendering and straining, add a little water to prevent scorching and bring to a boil in a flat-bottomed pot or kettle. Drop in the roulards, rolled and tied; stir with a spoon until well browned; then set back on the stove and let simmer gently for two hours with pot tightly covered. Drain well on napkin or sieve, and garnish with hard boiled eggs, parsley and slices of lemon. Serve hot. Each roulard should be about the size of an egg.

Mary E. Trautman

Beef Loaf.

From MRS. CARRINGTON MASON, of Tennessee, Alternate Lady Manager.

Three pounds lean finely chopped beef; one dozen rolled butter crackers; four beaten eggs; one tablespoonful black pepper; one tablespoonful salt; butter the size of an egg. Mix thoroughly, mold into two bricks and bake like a roast. This makes a very nice dish sliced cold for tea. A very little sage can be added if desired.

Mrs. Carrington Mason.

Hash.

From MRS. ANNIE L. Y. ORFF, of Missouri, Alternate Lady Manager.

Chop any kind of meat fine; to one cupful add one cup of chopped boiled potatoes, three-fourths cup bread crumbs, put one-half cup milk, one tablespoon butter, a little pepper and salt in a sauce pan on the stove; when boiling stir in the hash which should be well mixed together; take from the fire and add one well-beaten egg; heat gem pans, and grease; put a spoonful of the hash in each, and put in the oven till nicely browned.

Annie L. Y. Orff

Mutton Chops.

From Miss Mary B. Hancock, of Iowa, Treasurer of State Board and Alternate Lady Manager.

Sprinkle the chops with salt, pepper and flour; put them in the double broiler; broil over or before the fire for eight minutes. Serve on a *hot* dish with butter, salt, and pepper, or tomato sauce. The fire for chops should not be as hot as for steak. Chops can be seasoned with salt and pepper, wrapped in buttered paper, and broiled ten minutes over a hot fire.

Mary B. Hancock

Roast Lamb.

From Mrs. Robt. B. Mitchell, of Kansas, Lady Manager.

Brush three ounces of melted butter over the inner part of a well trimmed quarter of lamb, and strew thick with finely grated bread crumbs, seasoned with salt, pepper and parsley; roll and skewer four or five slices of bacon to the outer side; put in rather quick oven. When thoroughly done (not over cooked) remove the bacon and baste the meat with well beaten yolk of egg and gravy; cover thick with bread crumbs and brown nicely. Garnish the platter on which it is served with sprays of mint. Mint sauce should be an accompaniment. This makes not only an attractive looking, but delicious roast of lamb.

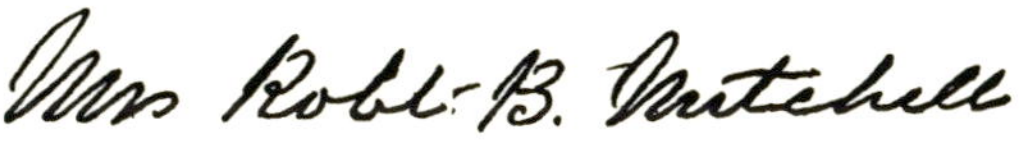

Lamb Chops.

From Mrs. Hester A. Hanback, of Kansas, Lady Manager.

Trim neatly and hack with sharp knife until tender; dip each piece in beaten egg and roll in cracker crumbs; place in pan equal quantities of butter and lard very hot; fry until nicely browned and serve with green peas.

Potted Tongue.

From Mrs. Frank H. Daniell, of New Hampshire, Alternate Lady Manager.

Take the remains of a cold boiled tongue, remove all the hard parts, cut the meat into small pieces and afterwards pound it to a smooth paste. Season with cayenne, and beat with it one-fourth of its weight in clarified butter. Press it into small jars, cover it one-fourth inch deep with clarified butter, melted drippings or melted suet. A smaller proportion of butter will be required if a little of the fat of the tongue is used instead of the lean only, but the butter must not be entirely dispensed with. It can be seasoned by the addition of one teaspoonful of mixed mustard, one salt spoonful of white pepper, a pinch of cayenne, and as much grated nutmeg as will cover a three-cent piece to each pound of tongue. Potted tongue is excellent when pounded with its weight in well dressed cold chicken, cold veal, or partridge. The tongue must be pounded to a perfectly smooth paste.

Mrs Frank H. Daniell.

Veal Croquettes.

From Mrs. Isabella Beecher Hooker, of Connecticut, Lady Manager.

Mince cold roast or boiled veal; add one-fourth as much of minced oysters scalded in their own liquor. Season with a dusting of red pepper, salt, a flavor of onion (two fine cut rounds of onion is sufficient), a tablespoonful of lemon juice. Stir this into a half pint of drawn butter made thick with flour; mould the croquettes; roll them in egg, then in cracker crumbs, salted and peppered; put them where they will be cold; when chilled put them in a frying basket into hot fat; two minutes will brown them.

Isabella Beecher Hooker

MISS KATHARINE L. MINOR.

Veal Croquettes.

From Miss Katharine L. Minor, of Louisiana, Fourth Vice President Board of Lady Managers.

Two pounds of veal, boiled until done; remove skin and bone and chop very fine; crumb a half loaf of bread and mix with the veal broth; add three eggs, two tablespoons of butter, salt, pepper, parsley, etc. Then form into egg-shaped balls and fry brown in boiling lard. It is necessary to dust the balls with cracker-dust or flour.

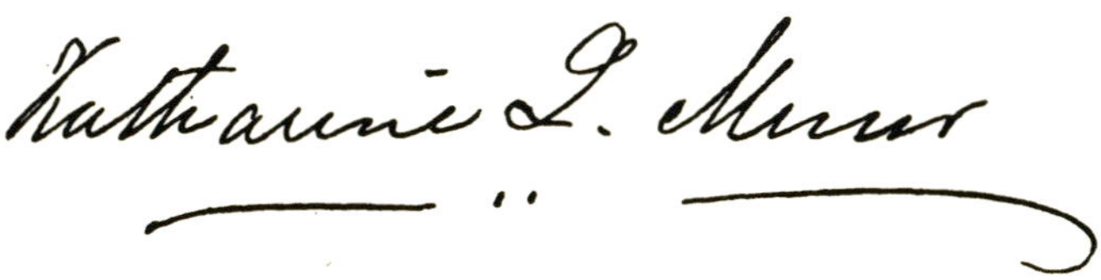

Veal-Pot Pie.

From Miss Susan W. Ball, of Indiana, Alternate Lady Manager.

Take two pounds of veal—a rib piece is good; cut it in small pieces; put it into a pot, having placed a small plate in the bottom to keep the meat from burning. Put in two quarts of water, either hot or cold. Keep it boiling for about an hour and a half. Then make a quart of flour into biscuit dough; drop in small lumps; cover closely. Twenty or twenty-five minutes will generally cook them. Be sure that there is water sufficient to cover the meat entirely when the dumplings are put in.

Casselettes de Veau.

From Mrs. James R. Deane, of California, Lady Manager.

This is a very simple, attractive and palatable dish for a luncheon table and may be used either warm or cold. Yours, cordially,

Mrs. James R. Deane

Ingredients for one dozen: One-quarter pound macaroni; one pound filet of veal; one ounce butter; one ounce flour; one gill of white stock or milk; three eggs; pepper; salt, and a little cayenne to taste. Chop the veal and then pass it twice through a sausage cutter or mincing machine. Cook the butter and flour together for about ten minutes; then add the milk or stock; then turn on a plate to cool; then add the minced veal; then add the seasoning; break the eggs in one by one; stir well. Boil the macaroni in salt and water until soft; drain it well and cut into rings about one-quarter inch long; have some small cups shaped like egg-cups; grease the sides slightly and place in the bottom of each cup a circular piece of cold boiled ham, fitting closely. Then arrange the macaroni on the sides, the open part to the side of the cup; then fill each cup with the chopped veal; cover with a greased paper and steam for twenty minutes. If eaten warm, use any gravy that may be used with veal. Will keep for two or three days.

Veal Fricassee.

From Mrs. T. J. Butler, of Arizona, Lady Manager.

Take a knuckle of veal; boil two hours in sufficient water to cover it; when thoroughly cooked, remove the meat and thicken the gravy with one tablespoonful of flour; add a little salt and one egg, well beaten; pour over the meat and serve hot with slices of lemon.

Mrs. T. J. Butler.

Veal Loaf.

From MRS. WHITING S. CLARK, of Iowa, Lady Manager.

Three pounds raw veal, chopped fine; two-thirds cup butter or its equivalent of salt pork, chopped; three eggs, well beaten with tablespoon milk; four Boston crackers, pounded fine; two even teaspoons pepper; one teaspoon sage; one tablespoon salt. Mix well in a loaf and bake two hours. Baste often with butter and water.

Mrs. Whiting S. Clark

Sweetbreads

Sweet-Bread Croquettes.

From Mrs. Schuyler Colfax, of Indiana, Alternate Lady Manager-at-Large.

It gives me great pleasure to send you the recipes you request, and thus further, in this small way, your unique and most generous project. The recipe for sweetbread croquettes is from Mrs. Henderson's Practical Cooking and Dinner Giving, but as it is the best one that I have ever tried, I send it. Cordially yours,

Ellen W. Colfax

Two pair of sweetbreads blanched and cut into dice. Half a box of mushrooms also cut into dice. Make a sauce by putting into a sauce pan one and a half ounces of butter, and when it bubbles, sprinkle in two ounces of flour, mix the butter and flour well together and cook thoroughly; then put in a gill of strong stock; stock for this is best made of chicken with some pieces of beef and veal added, or a gill of cream may be used instead of the stock. When the flour, butter and stock are well mixed, put in the sweetbreads and mushrooms and stir over the fire until they are thoroughly heated. Now take them off the fire, add the beaten yolks of two eggs, return to the fire long enough to set the eggs but do not allow them to boil. When cool, form into croquettes, roll first in cracker or bread crumbs, then in egg, and again in crumbs and fry in boiling lard.

Sweetbreads and Oysters.

From SEÑORA TERESA ARMIJO DE SYMINGTON, of New Mexico.

Soak and blanch your sweetbreads, cut them into equal sizes and remove the skins and little pipes. Take about three dozen fine oysters, strain off the liquor. Put the sweetbreads into a stew pan and cover them with the oyster liquor; add also, if you have it, three large spoonfuls of gravy of roast veal and a quarter of a pound of fresh butter cut into bits and each bit rolled in flour. When the sweetbreads are done put in the oysters and let them cook for about five minutes and take them out again; add at the last two wineglasses of sweet cream; stir up well for a few minutes and serve in a hot dish.

Sweetbreads and Mushrooms.

From MRS. P. B. WINSTON, of Minnesota, Alternate Lady Manager.

Take all the fat off sweetbreads; throw into boiling water; add one teaspoonful of salt and let stand on fire for twenty minutes; take from fire, remove all skin and pick to pieces. Put a tablespoonful of butter in a pan and let melt, add tablespoonful flour and one-half pint of cream; stir until it boils, add sweetbreads and five mushrooms chopped fine, one-half teaspoonful of salt and a little pepper. Serve in patties or paper cases.

Mrs P. B. Winston

Sweetbreads en Coquille.

From MISS JENNIE TORREYSON, of Nevada, Alternate Lady Manager.

One pound sweetbreads. Soak them one hour in salt water; boil till tender in salt water in which an onion has been put. One can mushrooms ("champignons") cut into small pieces, stew a bit till tender and mix with sweetbreads after they are boiled till tender and cut into small pieces. One pint cream, one tablespoonful butter, one tablespoonful flour. Cream the butter, mixing with the flour till smooth; stir with the cream, add one tablespoonful of Worcestershire sauce and stir together over the fire until it boils, then pour it over the sweetbreads and mushrooms. Serve in shells or cases. Can be used also without mushrooms if desired.

Jennie Torreyson

Sweetbread Patties.

From MISS WILHELMINE REITZ, of Indiana, Lady Manager.

Wash one pair of sweetbreads; throw them into boiling water and simmer gently twenty minutes; then throw them into cold water to blanch and cool. When cool pick them into small pieces, rejecting all the fine membrane. Chop fine a half can of mushrooms. Put a large tablespoonful of butter in a sauce pan to melt without browning; add an even tablespoonful of flour, mix until smooth; add a half pint of cream, stir continually until it boils; add a half teaspoonful of salt, a dash of white pepper; the mushrooms and sweetbreads mix and stand over boiling water for five minutes. Serve in paper cases, silver shells or in puff-paste cases.

POULTRY

Boiled Chicken.

From MRS. GOVERNOR EDWIN C. BURLEIGH, of Maine, Second Vice President Board of Lady Managers.

Joint the chicken; cut in small pieces; remove the skin; put into tepid water. Have ready a frying pan with hot melted butter; put the chicken into the pan and fry to a delicate brown; then put into a kettle, cover with water and boil very slowly for an hour. Season. Remove chicken and thicken gravy with flour.

Mrs. Edwin C. Burleigh

Jambolaya.

(A SPANISH CREOLE DISH.)

From MISS KATHARINE L. MINOR, of Louisiana, Fourth Vice President Board of Lady Managers.

Cut up the remains of a chicken or turkey, cover with water, and stew until the substance is extracted; then shred

MRS. EDWIN C. BURLEIGH.

the meat. Wash one pound of rice carefully and set aside. Put one tablespoon of lard into a porcelain-lined saucepan; add a small spoon of finely chopped onion and a tomato; then put in the shredded fowl and liquid in which it was boiled, adding the rice, red pepper and salt; sufficient water must be added to cover the rice, which must cook and steam until soft, but not wet or like mush.

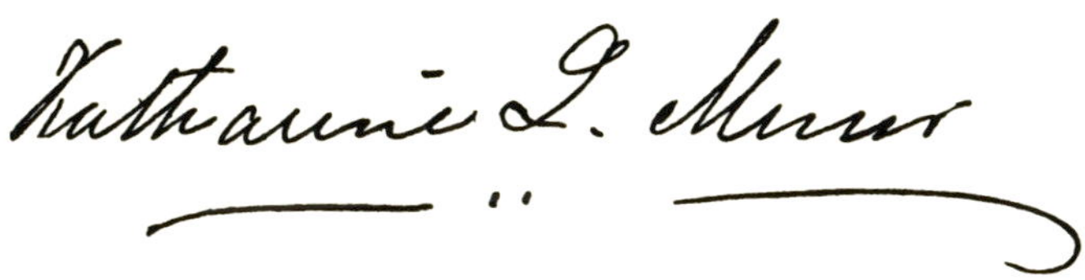

Chicken Livers, en brochette, with Bacon.

From MRS. COL. JAMES A. MULLIGAN, of Chicago, Lady Manager.

Take eighteen fresh chicken livers; dry well; season with pepper and salt; cut each liver in two pieces. Prepare six slices of lean bacon, broil one minute; cut each slice into six pieces. Take six silver skewers; run the skewer through the centre of the piece of chicken liver, then through a slice of bacon, until each skewer is filled with alternate slices of chicken liver and bacon. Roll each one in olive oil, then in bread crumbs, and broil five minutes on each side over moderate fire. Arrange on hot dish, pour Maître d'Hotel butter over them. Garnish with watercress and serve.

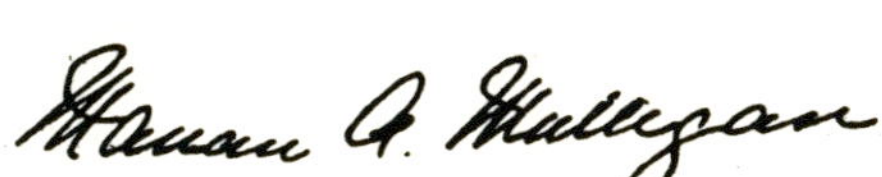

Pollo con Arroz.

From Señora Don Manuel Chaves, of New Mexico.

Primeramente se pone a herbir el pollo hasta que este bien cosido y despues se frie una poca de cobolla en manteca junto con el arroz y se le hecha pimienta entera y se le anade el caldo, colado, en que se cosio el pollo. Despues se anade el pollo cortado en pedazos pequeños y se le hecha sal.

Pollo con Tomates.

Lomismo que con arroz, con la excepcion que en lugar de arroz se le echan tomates.

Tamales de Chile.

Lomismo, con la excepcion que en lugar de echarles azucar, canela y pasas se les echa en el medio carne con chile y sal.

Coquilles de Volaille.

From Miss Josephine Shakspeare, of Louisiana, Lady Manager.

Boil the chicken until very tender; pull the meat from the bones in flakes; remove all the skin and cut the meat into very small pieces. Take one-half pint of the chicken broth, one teaspoonful of minced onion, the same of minced parsley, two tablespoons of butter rubbed into same quantity of flour, let this cook for a few moments and add one-half pint of cream or rich milk. Season the meat with a little cayenne pepper and some salt; add to this a small box of truffles, cut fine, also a box of mushrooms thinly sliced; stir all this into the sauce. If there should not be enough to cover the meat, add more broth, cream, butter and pepper, little by little, until you have enough sauce and of the right consistency. It should be as thick as rich cream. When cold add a claret glass of sherry wine. Before taking from the fire, add to it two more tablespoons of butter, a little at a time, never add all at once, it may oil it. Fill the shells, sprinkle bread crumbs on top and about twenty minutes before ready to serve them, place in a very hot oven to brown. Must not *stand after cooked.*

Josephine Shakespeare.

Croquettes.

From Mrs. L. C. Gillespie, of Tennessee, Lady Manager.

Breast of a large turkey; five sweetbreads; one and one-half pint of milk; one-half pound butter; five tablespoonfuls of flour; two eggs. Chop the turkey and sweetbreads very fine, using a silver knife for chopping the sweetbreads. Beat the whites and yolks of the eggs separately as you would for a cake. Mix the eggs, butter, flour and milk in a porcelain vessel and cook until the mixture comes to the consistency of cream sauce; and that it may cook smoothly, it will be necessary to make first a thick paste of the flour by stirring into it a very small quantity of the milk, gradually thinning it with more of the milk. While cooking it must be stirred constantly, and as soon as it is sufficiently thick add to the mixture the chopped turkey and sweetbreads and cook the whole for two minutes longer. Use no seasoning but pepper (white or cayenne) and salt to the taste. This quantity will make twenty-two large croquettes, which are prettiest moulded in a pear-shaped wine glass. With a little practice you can mould them in your hand. Have ready some cracker crumbs rolled very fine and dust like. Fry the croquettes in boiling lard and enough to cover them. When a rich brown take them out and place on sieve or brown paper to rid them of the surplus grease. Run them into a well heated oven for a few minutes before serving. Put a teaspoonful of cream sauce on the top of each croquette.

Mrs L. C. Gillespie

Chicken Croquettes.

From Mrs. Sarah H. Bixby, of Maine, Alternate Lady Manager.

Chop one-half pound chicken quite fine; add one teaspoonful salt; one saltspoonful pepper; one saltspoonful celery salt; one teaspoon lemon juice; one tablespoon chopped parsley and a few drops of onion juice; moisten with the thick cream sauce.

Thick Cream Sauce—Melt two tablespoons butter; add two heaping tablespoons cornstarch; one teaspoon salt and one saltspoon pepper; add slowly one pint hot cream and beat well.

Sarah H. Bixby

Curry of Chicken in Puffs.

From Señora Teresa Armijo de Symington, of New Mexico.

First prepare your puffs by the following recipe. Ingredients: Two cupfuls of milk, two of flour, two eggs and a piece of butter the size of an egg melted; a little salt; beat the eggs separately and well; add the milk to the yolks, then the flour and so on, the whites last; beat all well together. They may be baked in teacups. This quantity will make about a dozen puffs.

Curry of Chicken—Buy a young chicken, cut it into pieces, leaving out all the bones; season with pepper and salt to taste; fry them in butter until well done; cut an onion fine, which fry in the same butter until brown; add a teacupful of clear stock, a teaspoonful of sugar. Take about a tablespoonful of curry powder and a little flour, mix and rub together with a little of the stock until quite smooth; add to the sauce pan; put in the chicken and let it boil for a few minutes; just before taking out add the juice of half a lemon. When this is all ready proceed to fill puffs while hot and serve immediately. Garnish puffs with parsley and serve a dish of cold slaw with it.

Pilauf.

From Miss Floride Cuningham, of South Carolina, Lady Manager.

Select a good fat hen, one pound of bacon strip, and one dozen whole black peppers, and boil together until quite done. Take them out of the pot, and put into the liquid left a pint and a half of rice, seasoned with a dessertspoonful of salt, boil twenty minutes, drain from it any of the juice that may remain, and place the pot again on the range, where the rice cannot burn, but where it will have the opportunity to dry thoroughly—each grain remaining apart. Keep the chicken hot and brown the bacon in the oven. When the rice is ready serve in an open dish, place the chicken on the top and pour over it a rich sauce of melted butter and hard boiled eggs chopped fine. The bacon can be sliced very thin and served with lettuce as a course.

Floride Cunningham

Fricassee Chicken.

From MRS. HELEN C. BRAYTON, of South Carolina, Vice-President of State Board and Lady Manager.

Cut the chicken in pieces and stew in as much water as will cover it. Add a bunch of sweet herbs, white pepper and onions. When cooked, add the yolks of six eggs, glass of white wine, chopped parsley, butter, and tablespoonful of cream, all beaten together.

Helen C Brayton

A Good Roast Turkey.

From MRS. HELEN A. PECK, of Missouri, Alternate Lady Manager-at-Large.

An ordinary turkey weighing eight to ten pounds requires at least two hours for proper and thorough cooking. Prepare your fowl and rub dry with a clean towel; then mix a little pepper and salt and rub both inside and outside of the turkey before putting in the dressing. Grate stale bread, about three cups; then add a small teaspoon of pepper and the same amount of powdered sage or sweet marjoram, salt and a little salt fat pork chopped very fine or a piece of butter the size of an egg; use warm water to mix the whole to the consistency of thick batter; beat an egg and stir into it the last thing; stuff the breast with half of the dressing, then sew up with coarse white thread and put the remaining dressing into the body and sew up. Take skewers of wood or iron and pin the wings closely to the sides, then turn the neck back and pin that firmly. One can use twine and tie them if they haven't the skewers. Force the legs down and tie tightly to the body before placing the turkey in the dripping pan with nearly a pint of water. Have a brisk fire and baste the turkey at least every fifteen minutes with these drippings. This frequent basting is of great importance as it keeps in the juices and allows thorough cooking. Turn the turkey two or three times during the cooking. During the last half hour dredge with flour and butter freely. The crisp pasty look so desirable and appetizing comes from this. Cook gizzard and liver in a sauce pan on the stove until thoroughly tender, then chop very fine and put them in the gravy to boil thoroughly in the dripping pan in the gravy which is delicious, and to be served from a tureen.

Helen A. Peck

Dressing for Turkey.

From Mrs. W. H. Felton, of Georgia, Lady Manager.

Bread crumbs and cold rice, equal quantities; season with pepper, onion and salt to taste, mixing well with cup of butter and yolks of three hard boiled eggs; dress the outside with circles of white hard boiled eggs and sprigs of parsley or celery.

Mrs. W. H. Felton

How to Cook Chestnuts.

From Miss Eloise L. Roman, of Maryland, Alternate Lady Manager.

Two quarts of water to one quart of fresh chestnuts. If dried they should be soaked several hours in cold water. Boil from three - quarters to one hour. Abut five minutes before they are done add a handful of salt. Peel and skin, serve hot, browned in butter, or cold with salad dressing and equal parts of chopped celery. When parboiled and skinned with salt and a little pepper it makes an excellent dressing for turkeys.

Eloise L. Roman

GAME

Wild Duck in Maryland.

From Mrs. William Reed, of Maryland, Lady Manager.

Wild ducks, canvassback, redheads, etc., are roasted without stuffing. After they are picked and thoroughly cleansed, roast them in a tin kitchen before a hot fire or in a quick oven for twenty-one minutes. They should be well browned on the outside, but the blood should run when cut with a knife. Unless underdone the flavor of the duck is destroyed. Fried hominy is generally served with wild duck; and fresh celery. Currant jelly is sometimes used.

Mrs William Reed

Snipe and Woodcock Broiled on Toast.

From Mrs. Rufus S. Frost, of Massachusetts, Lady Manager.

Prepare the birds with great care; place in baking tin and put in oven. Pour into the tin enough water, boiling hot, to cover the bottom of the tin or bake pan; cover the bake pan with another tin; keep them closely covered and let them cook very steadily until tender, adding from time to time enough boiling hot water to keep birds from burning, or even *sticking* to the tin. When very tender remove from the oven and from the bake pan, carefully saving all the liquid in the pan, which you set on top of the stove, which is the foundation and the *flavor* for your sauce or gravy which you make *in this* pan for your birds after they are broiled. Have in an earthen dish some melted butter; dip the birds in the butter and then in Indian or corn meal and put on the gridiron to brown and finish cooking; keep them hot as possible until you serve. Arrange nicely trimmed pieces of toasted bread on the heated platter, put on each piece a bird, pour over and around the birds on the platter a sauce which you make *in* the bake pan in which your birds were semi-cooked, and which you have kept on top of the range while your birds were broiling. Pour into this pan of *liquid* or "juice" one teacup sweet cream, and thicken with one tablespoon butter, yolk of one egg and two tablespoons of Indian meal; let it boil up once just to thicken, and pour boiling hot onto the birds and toast on platter, saving some to send in in separate serving dish. If you prefer flour to the corn meal to dip the birds in after the melted butter bath, use flour also to thicken the sauce or gravy, which should be a brown sauce or gravy and is generally brown enough if made in roasting pan. A prize cook in Washington once confided to me that "a leetle last year's spiced pickle syrup am luscious flavor for gravy of the wee birds, robins, quail, snipe and them like." Alas! In the same moment of flattering triumph for *me*, she added — triumphantly on *her* part also — "Lor, chile, I'se de only one libing dis day dat knows nuff to use that same, sure!"

Mrs Rufus S. Frost

MRS. WILLIAM REED.

Prairie Chicken.

From Mrs. E. S. Thomson, of Maryland, Lady Manager.

Do not wash prairie chickens. Cover the breasts with very thin slices of bacon, or rub them well with butter; roast them before a good fire, basting them often with butter. Cook twenty minutes, salt and pepper them, and serve on a hot dish as soon as cooked.

Sauce for the above—First roll a pint of dry bread crumbs and pass half of them through a sieve. Put a small onion into a pint of milk and when it boils remove the onion and thicken the milk with the half pint of sifted crumbs; take from the fire and stir in a heaping teaspoonful of butter, a grating of nutmeg, pepper and salt. Put a little butter in a sautée pan, and when hot throw in the half pint of coarser crumbs which remained in the sieve; stir them over the fire until they assume a light brown color, taking care that they do not burn, and stir into them a pinch of cayenne pepper. For serving, pour over the chicken, when helped, a spoonful of the white sauce and on this place a spoonful of the crumbs.

E. S. Thomson

VEGETABLES

Vegetable Oyster.

From Mrs. Governor Bagley, of Michigan, Lady Manager-at-Large.

I regret that the long distance I am from home prevents me from sending you many valuable recipes I would be glad to contribute to your book. One, however, occurs to me that you may consider worthy a place, and, I assure you, makes a very delicious dish.

Sincerely yours,

Frances E. N. Bagley

While cooking vegetable oyster put in the kettle a small piece of codfish. This adds very much to its flavor and delicacy and makes a delicious dish out of what would otherwise be an almost tasteless vegetable. The codfish should, of course, be removed before sending to the table.

Cauliflower with Tartar Sauce.

From Mrs. Myra Bradwell, of Chicago, Lady Manager.

Serve the cauliflower with one cup of drawn butter in which has been stirred the juice of a lemon, and a half teaspoonful of French mustard, mixed up well with the sauce.

Myra Bradwell

Scalloped Potatoes.

From Mrs. Beriah Wilkins, of District of Columbia, Fifth Vice-President, Board of Lady Managers.

Slice six raw potatoes as thin as wafers. This can be done with a sharp knife, although there is a little instrument for the purpose, to be had at the house furnishing stores, which flutes prettily as well as slices evenly. Lay in ice water a few minutes; then put a layer in the bottom of a pudding dish, and over this sprinkle salt and pepper and small bits of butter; then another layer of potatoes and so on until the dish is full. Pour over this a pint of milk, stick bits of butter thickly over it, cover the dish, set it in the oven, bake half an hour. Remove the cover if not sufficiently brown.

Mrs Beriah Wilkins

Escalloped Sweet Potatoes.

From Mrs. P. B. Winston, of Minnesota, Alternate Lady Manager.

Take large sweet potatoes; parboil them slightly and cut them in transverse slices. Prepare a deep baking dish and cover the bottom with a layer of slices; add a little butter, a very little sugar and nutmeg. Strew over this a few bits of orange peel and add a little juice of the orange. Fill the dish in like manner, finishing with fine shred of orange peel. Bake until tender and you will have a dish to satisfy an epicure.

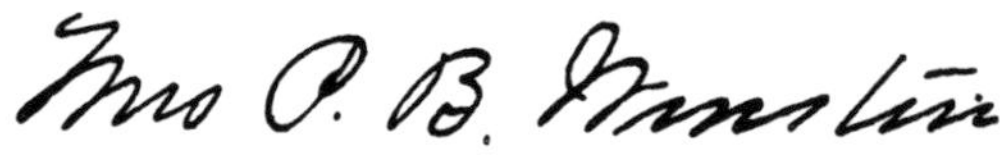

Potato Puff.

(A LA GENEVE.)

From MRS. H. F. BROWN, of Minnesota, Lady Manager.

Whip mashed potatoes light and soft, with milk, butter and two raw eggs; season with pepper and salt, and beat in a few spoonfuls of powdered cheese. Pile upon a bake-dish and brown nicely. Serve in dish.

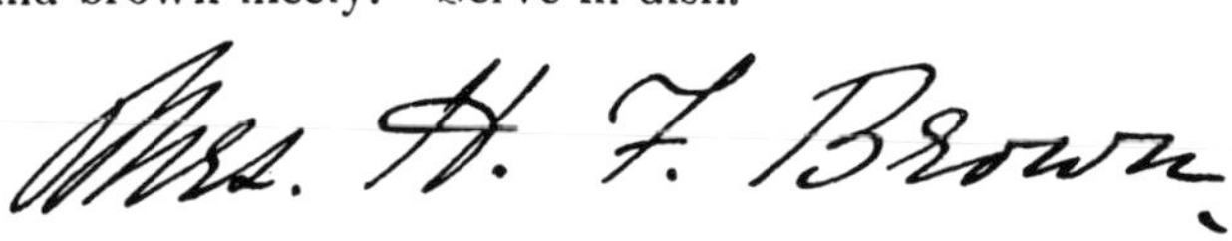

Potato Croquettes.

From MRS. FRANCES P. BURROWS, of Michigan, Alternate Lady Manager.

Four large mealy potatoes, cold. Mash them; add two tablespoons of fresh, melted butter, pinch of salt, a little pepper, one tablespoon of cream. Whip it for about five minutes or until very smooth and light. Make into forms, roll them in a beaten egg and bread crumbs. Fry in boiling lard.

Potatoes — Mashed.

From Mrs. E. J. P. Howes, of Michigan, Lady Manager.

Peel potatoes thin; put into boiling water with a little salt added. Cook until tender; drain off the water and remove the cover a few moments to dry the potatoes; turn into an earthen dish that has been heated, and beat up with a wire beater or silver fork, moistening the whole with cream; or, if not available, milk with a little butter will answer; salt to taste and mold in any desired form when it is ready to serve. A wooden masher is apt to make it heavy, while beating will make it light and creamy.

E. J. P. Howes

Boston Baked Beans.

From Mrs. Elizabeth C. Langworthy, of Nebraska, Lady Manager.

Soak one quart of small, dry beans over night. Parboil in the morning and place in earthen jar, with salt and pepper to taste. Add one-half teaspoon soda and two tablespoons of molasses; also a small piece of salt pork. Cover with water and bake eight hours, adding boiling water as needed.

Elizabeth C. Langworthy

Lima Beans.

From Mrs. Mariam D. Cooper, of Montana, Alternate Lady Manager.

Soak beans over night; cook one hour in water, leaving very little water when done. Just before serving season with pepper, salt, cream and butter and heat thoroughly.

Baked Tomatoes.

From Mrs. Governor Rickards, of Montana, President State Board and Lady Manager.

Select large-sized, smooth and round tomatoes. Cut from the stem end a slice and lay aside. Scoop all the inside of tomato out, being careful not to break through; add half as much cracker or bread crumbs; season highly with salt and pepper; add plenty of butter, a dash or two of cayenne; put on the stove and cook for ten minutes. Now fill the hollow tomatoes with this dressing; when full, add four or six whole cloves, putting them on top of the dressing; either pile up high or make level and put on the sliced top. Place tomatoes in a large baking pan, with a little hot water to prevent sticking. Bake fifteen minutes.

COUNTESS OF ABERDEEN, MEMBER OF THE WOMEN'S COMMITTEE OF LONDON FOR THE WORLD'S COLUMBIAN EXPOSITION.

Baked Tomatoes.

From MRS. AUGUSTA TRUMAN, of California, Lady Alternate-at-Large.

Select smooth, medium-sized tomatoes; make a small aperture at the stalk end; remove the pulp and seeds with a spoon and put into a sieve to drain. Chop equal parts of cold chicken and veal and one green pepper; add a well-beaten egg, half cup grated bread crumbs, piece of butter, pepper, salt, sage and a suspicion of onion; mix well together; moisten with some of the juice; fill the tomatoes; bake half an hour in a moderate oven. Serve each tomato on a lettuce leaf. This makes a pretty as well as a savory entrée.

Stewed Tomatoes.

From MISS MARY H. KROUT, of Indiana, Alternate Lady Manager.

Take one quart of firm ripe tomatoes; stew one hour and a half over an even fire and stir frequently to prevent scorching; then add half a cup of bread crumbs, one teaspoonful of sugar, salt to taste, a pinch of cayenne pepper, a heaping tablespoonful of good butter and half a cup of sweet cream. Boil together twenty minutes and serve hot.

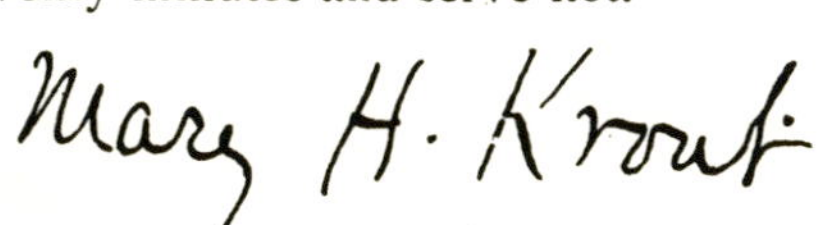

Beets.

From Mrs. Governor John M. Stone, of Mississippi, Lady Manager.

Boil until perfectly done; then pour melted butter, salt and pepper over and serve hot.

Mrs John M. Stone.

Parsnips — Stewed.

From Mrs. M. R. Lee, of Mississippi, Lady Manager.

Wash, scrape, and slice about half an inch thick; have a skillet prepared with half pint hot water and a tablespoon butter; add the parsnips, season with salt and pepper, cover closely and stew until the water is cooked away, stirring occasionally to prevent burning. When done the parsnips will be of a creamy, light brown color.

M R. Lee

Stuffed Green Peppers.

From Mrs. Alice B. Castleman, of Kentucky, Alternate Lady Manager.

Cut off the small end of the pepper; make a slit down the side; remove all the seeds. Mince fine cold chicken, veal or shrimps, and add a little stale bread soaked in water and well squeezed to dry it; one-half teaspoonful minced onion; a little minced parsley, pepper, salt and one tablespoonful of butter. Put a large tablespoonful of butter in a spider and heat the dressing for the peppers in it for a few minutes; then stuff them, tie on the tops and the sides together also. In a sauce pan put a heaping tablespoonful of butter; when hot add one-half tablespoonful of flour, which brown in the butter; add a little onion minced fine and a cup of water; put in the peppers, cover closely and let them simmer slowly until tender; when done, add one tablespoonful of butter, pepper and salt to taste.

Corn Oysters.

From Mrs. John S. Briggs, of Nebraska, Lady Manager.

One teacup milk, three eggs, one pint green corn grated very fine, a little salt and as much flour as will make a slightly stiff batter; beat the eggs, the yolks and whites separately. To the yolks of the eggs add the milk, corn, salt and flour; beat the whole very hard, then stir in the whites of the eggs and the oysters; after having dredged them in a portion of the grated corn, drop this batter, a spoonful at a time, into hot lard and fry until done.

Fried Egg Plant.

From Mrs. Lily Rosecrans Toole, of Montana, Lady Manager.

Pare the egg plant and cut in very thin slices; sprinkle each slice with salt and pepper; pile them evenly; put a tin plate over them and on this stand a flatiron to press out the juice. Let stand one hour. Beat an egg lightly and add to it a tablespoonful of boiling water; dip each slice first in this and then in bread crumbs. Put three tablespoonfuls of lard into a frying pan; when hot sauté the slices, a few at a time; brown one side then turn and brown the other. As the fat is consumed add more, waiting each time for it to heat before putting in the egg plant. Drain on brown paper and serve very hot. Tomato catsup should be served with it. (*Mrs. Rohrer's Cook Book.*)

Macaroni – Good.

From Mrs. Sam S. Fifield, of Wisconsin, Alternate Lady Manager.

Five tablespoons of grated cheese, one of flour, one of butter, one egg, one-half cup of cream, salt and pepper; put over the fire and stir until the cheese is dissolved. Boil one-fourth package of macaroni in salted water about fifteen minutes, drain, cover with milk and boil again. Stir all together and bake until brown.

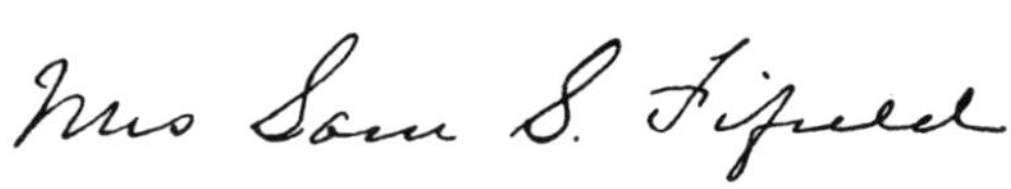

Rice as a Vegetable.

From Mrs. Charles H. Olmstead, of Georgia, Lady Manager.

Wash and pick thoroughly one quart of rice; put in pot containing two quarts of boiling water; salt to taste; let the rice boil for fifteen minutes; then pour off all the water that has not been absorbed by the rice and place the pot on back of stove to steam; stir occasionally until grains of rice separate.

Mrs Charles H Olmsted

Cranberries.

From Mrs. Lana A. Bates, of Nebraska, Alternate Lady Manager.

After removing all soft berries, wash thoroughly; place for about two minutes in scalding water, remove, and to every pound of fruit add three-quarters of a pound of granulated sugar and a half pint of water: stew together over a moderate but steady fire. Be careful to *cover* and *not stir* the fruit, but shake the vessel. If attention to these particulars be given the berries will retain their shape to quite an extent, which materially adds to their appearance on the table. Boil from five to seven minutes; remove from the fire; turn into a deep dish, and set aside to cool. If strained sauce be preferred, one and a half pounds of fruit should be stewed in one pint of water for ten or fifteen minutes or until quite soft; then strain through a colander or fine wire sieve; add three quarters of a pound of sugar and return to the fire and boil three minutes, stirring constantly; set away to cool, when it will be ready for use.

Lana A. Bates

EGGS

Plain Omelet with Eight Eggs.

From Mrs. L. Brace Shattuck, of Chicago, Lady Manager.

Beat separately and very lightly the whites and yolks of eight eggs. To one tablespoon of flour add one-half teaspoon of baking powder and one-half cup of sweet milk. Add the beaten yolks and lastly the beaten whites of the eggs. Have ready a hot frying pan, with a generous amount of melted butter, into which pour, a cupful at a time, the mixture. As soon as it *sets*, lift carefully the one half over upon the other, and when done remove to a hot plate and serve immediately. This omelet is exceedingly light and is sufficient for four or five persons.

Mrs. L. Brace Shattuck

Green Corn Omelet.

From Mrs. Frances P. Burrows, of Michigan, Alternate Lady Manager.

Grate twelve ears of boiled corn. Beat five eggs until light and stir into the corn; season with pepper and salt, and one tablespoon butter; fry until brown. If fried in small cakes with a little flour and milk stirred in to make a batter, it will be found excellent.

Omelet with Ham.

From Mrs. Naomi T. Compton, of New Jersey, Alternate Lady Manager.

Have a teacupful of very finely minced ham prepared for use as soon as the eggs are ready. Beat the whites of eight eggs separately and have the yolks beaten the same length of time as the whites. We always put the eggs in the refrigerator over night if the omelet is to be used for breakfast, for the eggs will beat much better if thoroughly cold. We use the same amount of flour and milk as of ham, but moisten the flour with milk until it is of the consistency of cream, pouring in the milk and flour with the yolks of the eggs. Add lastly the whites, beaten stiff, alternating with the finely minced ham and whites, until all are combined. Do not stir around in one direction, but lift the yellow mixture up through and into the white. Get it into the oven as soon as possible, which must be blazing hot. If baked in a bread tin it will usually rise to double the amount. If you prefer baking on the top of a stove, have your frying pan hot, with plenty of butter, and turn the omelet as soon as the edges are cooked. Great care must be taken not to have the pan keep too hot after the cooking begins, for nothing burns so quickly as egg, and if scorched the delicate flavor is lost. Plain flour can be used with the proper proportions of baking powder.

Omelet must be eaten directly after it comes from the

fire to be tasted at its best. A little chopped parsley may be added as a flavoring, but it need not be chopped so finely as the ham.

Naomi T. Compton.

Omelet—Plain.

From Miss Mary E. Busselle, of New Jersey, Lady Manager.

Four eggs, well beaten; four tablespoons milk; two tablespoons melted butter. Bake in a quick oven, in buttered round jelly tins, and when browned, turn half over and send to the table hot.

Mary E. Busselle.

Stuffed Eggs.

From Mrs. Ralph Trautmann, of New York City, First Vice-President Board of Lady Managers.

Boil twelve eggs for twenty minutes; cut in halves; take out the yolks and mash to a paste, adding one onion chopped fine, butter size of an egg, one-half cup of milk, a little chopped parsley, with salt and pepper to taste. Mix well; roll this paste into balls and refill the empty halves, joining the cut eggs together again with the white of a raw egg. Roll the stuffed eggs in beaten yolk and cracker crumbs, and brown in boiling lard, same as crullers. Drain well and serve on toast or lettuce leaves.

Mary E. Trautmann

MRS. RALPH TRAUTMANN.

Deviled Eggs for Luncheon or Picnics.

From Mrs. Isabella Laning Candee, of Illinois, Alternate Lady Manager.

Boil any number of eggs very hard, turning over carefully in the water several times to prevent their being unevenly cooked; put into cold water a few moments and then take off shells; cut in halves carefully and take out the yolks; mash these fine with a silver spoon (use a *silver* knife for cutting and filling) and add to them as much good mayonnaise dressing as may be required to make a smooth paste with which fill the empty halves; put them evenly together, fasten with toothpicks, and wrap each egg in white tissue paper and put in the ice chest until ready to serve.

Isabella Laning Candee

Escalloped Eggs.

From Mrs. Helen A. Peck, of Missouri, Alternate Lady Manager-at-Large.

Escalloped eggs makes a savory dish and this is how to prepare them: Put half a dozen eggs into a sauce pan of boiling water and keep the pan where it will be hot for half an hour, but not where the water will boil. At the end of the prescribed time lay the eggs in cold water for five minutes, and then remove the shells. Cut the whites into thin slices and rub the yolks through a coarse sieve. Mix both parts lightly, and after putting the mixture into an escallop dish pour over it a sauce made as follows: Put two tablespoonfuls of butter into a frying pan, and when it has been melted add a heaping tablespoonful of flour. Stir until the mixture is smooth and frothy, then gradually add a pint of cold milk. Boil up once and season with salt and pepper. After pouring the sauce over the eggs spread a large cupful of grated bread crumbs on top of the dish and cook for fifteen minutes in a hot oven. If care be taken to prevent the eggs from boiling at any time during the thirty minutes the dish will be delicate and digestible.

Helen A. Peck

How to Take Egg.

From Mrs. Naomi T. Compton, of New Jersey, Alternate Lady Manager.

Have never seen this recipe for preparing an egg for invalids or convalescents, so I venture to add it on account of its excellence. Some people dislike the taste of raw egg, and would find it palatable in other ways than beaten up with wine, or taken in a glass of sweetened milk. Prepare a cup of coffee to the taste, with cream and sugar, keeping it very hot until ready for the egg, which must be beaten thoroughly in another cup, and the prepared coffee added by degrees to the egg; drink it hot, and you will never want to take coffee again without the addition of egg.

Naomi T. Compton.

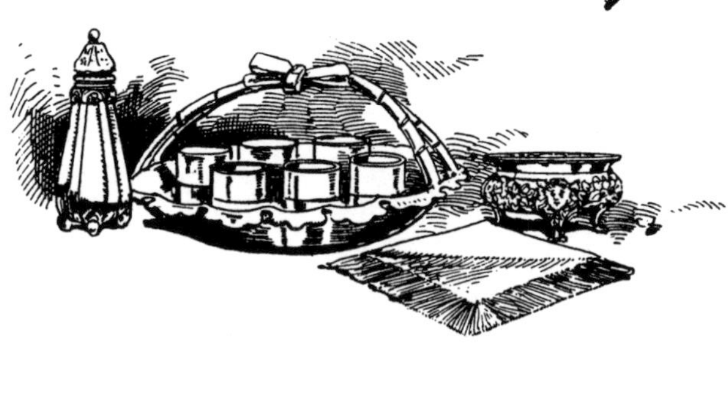

Lobster Salad.

From Mrs. Charles Price, of North Carolina, Third Vice President, Board of Lady Managers.

Lobsters are done when they assume a red color, which will only require a few minutes hard boiling. Remove the skin and bones, pick to pieces with a fork, marinate them, *i. e.*, place in a dish and season with salt, pepper and a little oil, plenty of vinegar and a little onion cut up; then cover and let stand two or three hours. Cut up hard boiled eggs for a border, line the bottom of the dish with lettuce leaves, place the lobster on the dish in a ring. Mayonnaise can be used if desired, but the lobster is excellent without it.

Mrs Charles Price

Chicken Salad.

From Mrs. A. M. Palmer, of New York, Alternate Lady Manager.

Ingredients: One fowl (boiled); one cucumber; two heads lettuce; two beets (boiled). Dressing made according to the following recipe: One teaspoonful mixed mustard;

one-half teaspoonful sugar; four tablespoonfuls salad oil; four tablespoonfuls milk; two tablespoonfuls vinegar; cayenne and salt to taste; add the oil, drop by drop, to the mustard and sugar, mixing carefully; next add milk and vinegar *very gradually*, lest the sauce curdle, and the seasoning. Place the shredded chicken on a bed of lettuce, and pour the dressing over it. Around the edge arrange rings of hard boiled eggs, sliced cucumber and beet root.

Mrs A. M. Palmer

Southern Chicken Salad.

SPLENDID—TRY IT ONCE.

From MRS. CHARLES J. McCLUNG, of Tennessee, Alternate Lady Manager.

Cut one chicken into small pieces (not too small); boil *one* egg hard and pulverize the yolk (cut the white into the chicken); add the beaten yolks of *three* raw eggs; one-half teaspoonful each of ground mustard, white pepper, salt, sugar and celery salt or seed, the juice of one lemon, one tablespoonful melted butter, one tablespoonful salad oil (some prefer all butter); beat all well together until light and pour into one gill of boiling vinegar and let all cook until thick as cream, stirring constantly to avoid curdling. When *cold* pour over your chicken, to which has been added as much chopped celery, and salt and pepper to taste.

Mrs Charles J. McClung

Chicken Salad.

From MRS. MARGARET M. RATCLIFFE, of Arkansas, Alternate Lady Manager.

As the Irishman would say, turkey makes the best chicken salad. Boil till well done. Use only the white meat, which cut with sharp scissors into pieces about one-half inch square; add an equal quantity of celery cut in same manner, sprinkling over it salt and pepper. Put in a cold place till two hours before serving, when add the following dressing: For one chicken take three eggs, one cup of vinegar, one cup of sweet milk, one-half cup butter, one tablespoon made mustard, salt, black and red pepper, beat eggs, melt butter; stir all together over a slow fire till it thickens; when cool beat into it one cup of cream. Serve salad on crisp, well-bleached lettuce leaves, on the top of each putting a small quantity of the following mayonnaise dressing: The yolks of two uncooked eggs, one tablespoon salt, beat with an eggbeater, adding gradually pure olive oil till one pint is used. When the mixture becomes too thick add, as required, one teaspoon of vinegar or lemon juice. If the oil is well incorporated by thorough beating, this dressing will keep an indefinite time.

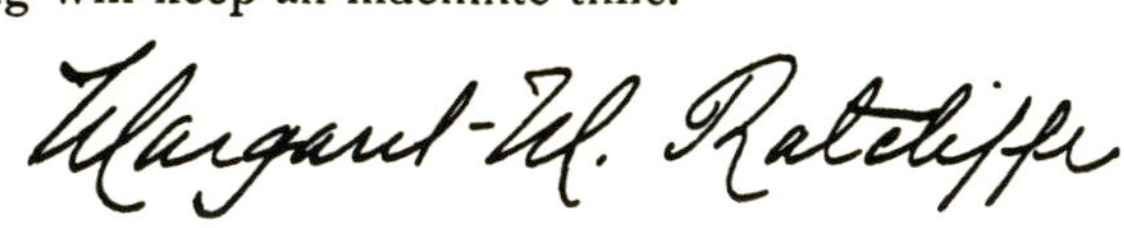

Vegetable Salad.

From MRS. FLORENCE H. KIDDER, of North Carolina, Lady Manager.

One pint of cold boiled potatoes, cut in slices; one-third the quantity of cold boiled beets cut *fine*; one-third the quantity of green peas (winter beets and canned peas are as good as fresh ones); sprinkle with salt and pepper, then pour over it a French dressing made of a saltspoonful of salt, one of black pepper, a teaspoonful of onion juice or grated onion, three tablespoonfuls of olive oil and one of vinegar; mix thoroughly and set aside. When ready to serve spread over it a thick mayonnaise dressing and garnish with slices of beet, cut in shapes, hard boiled egg and parsley; if made in summer a border of crisp lettuce leaves is an additional garnish. If the quantity of vegetable is increased the amount of dressing must also be doubled or the salad will be dry. A small portion of the mayonnaise mixed with the vegetables also is an improvement.

String Bean Salad.

(FRENCH RECIPE.)

From Mrs. Caroline E. Dennis, of New York State, Alternate Lady Manager-at-Large.

String the beans and boil them whole; when boiled tender and they have become cold, slice them lengthwise, cutting each bean into four long slices; season them an hour or two before serving, with a marinade of a little pepper, salt, and three spoonfuls of vinegar to one spoonful of oil. Just before serving, drain from them any drops of superfluous liquid that may have collected and carefully mix them with a French dressing. This makes a delicious salad.

French Salad Dressing—One tablespoon of vinegar; three tablespoons of olive oil; one saltspoon of pepper, and one saltspoon of salt. (This is half a spoon too much

MRS. LAURA E. HOWEY.

pepper for Americans.) Add a trifle of onion, scraped fine, or rubbed on the salad bowl, if it is desired at all. Pour the oil, mixed with the pepper and salt, over the salad; mix them well together; then add the vinegar, and mix again. Serve on a leaf of crisp lettuce.

Caroline E. Dennis.

Excellent Potato Salad.

From Mrs. Genevieve M. Guthrie, of Oklahoma, Lady Manager.

For four or six people. Cut into dice six medium sized potatoes (boiled); three medium onions; salt and pepper them to taste; pour over and mix well the following dressing: Three well beaten eggs, three large tablespoonfuls of strong vinegar, a lump of butter size of a walnut, pinch of salt, pepper and mustard (unmixed); put on the stove and cook to a thin custard, stirring constantly.

Mrs Genevieve M Guthrie

Tomato Salad.

From Mrs. Mira B. F. Ladd, of New Hampshire, Lady Manager.

Six tomatoes, one-half cup of mayonnaise dressing, the crisp part of one head of lettuce. Peel the tomatoes and put them on the ice until they are very cold; make the mayonnaise and stand it on the ice until wanted; wash and dry the lettuce. When ready to serve, cut the tomatoes in halves, make twelve little nests with two or three salad leaves each, arrange on the dish, place half a tomato in each nest, put a tablespoonful of mayonnaise on each tomato and serve immediately.

Mrs. D. F. Ladd.

Tomato Salad.

(FOR USE WHEN FRESH TOMATOES ARE NOT IN THE MARKET.)

From MISS MARY CREASE SEARS, of Massachusetts, Alternate Lady Manager.

Rub through a coarse sieve one can of tomatoes; cover with cold water a half box of Cox gelatine and let it stand a half hour or more; then pour in enough hot water to thoroughly dissolve it; then mix with one full pint of the strained tomatoes; add a little salt; pour into small round moulds and put in a cool place to harden. Serve on lettuce leaves with mayonnaise dressing.

Mary Crease Sears

Cabbage Salad.

From MRS. THERESA J. COCHRAN, of Vermont, Alternate Lady Manager.

Mix together one-half cup of sugar, one teaspoonful of mustard, one teaspoonful of salt, one-half teaspoonful black pepper; then add three well beaten eggs, one-half cup of vinegar, six tablespoonfuls of cream, three of butter. Cook the same as boiled custard in a kettle of water; when cold add the cabbage chopped fine.

Theresa J Cochran

Fish Salad.

From Mrs. Mary C. Bell, of Florida, Lady Manager.

Pour boiling water over a large mackerel and let stand for ten minutes; take out and dry thoroughly by draining on a sieve or clean towel. Remove the head, tail and fins, and skin and bones. Shred the fish finely and mix with one large onion, well chopped. Add mustard, vinegar, and pepper to taste. Serve as salad, with young lettuce leaves, and garnish with hard-boiled eggs, sliced. This is a delightful relish with thin-sliced bread and butter, and is called "Salmagundi."

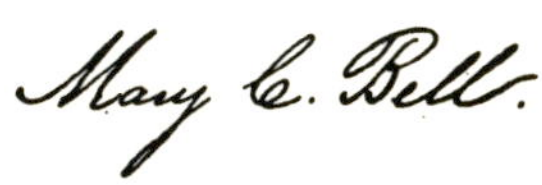

Salad Dressing.

From Miss Loraine Pearce Bucklin, of Rhode Island, Alternate Lady Manager.

Three eggs, beat yolks and whites separately. To the beaten yolks add one tablespoonful of mustard, two tablespoonfuls of sugar, one teaspoonful of salt. To the beaten whites of the eggs add one cup of cream; beat this thoroughly together, pour the yolks, mustard, sugar and salt into this and put the dish containing it over the teakettle when the water boils. When the mixture begins to harden around the edge, pour in a cup of vinegar; stir it all the time it is over the kettle. After you add the vinegar take it from the heat and set in a dish of cold water to cool.

DOUGHNUTS & FRITTERS

Famous Doughnuts.

From Miss Frances E. Willard, of Illinois, Lady Manager.

To tell you the truth, I never knew anything about cooking or had a particle of taste for it, but I will send you the recipe for her famous 'doughnuts,' written out by my beloved mother, and I think about the last communication she ever prepared for the press; it was in March of last year. There is nothing specially valuable about the recipe except that it is good and decidedly old-fashioned. I used to think there was nothing so toothsome as mother's 'fried cakes,' for so we called them on the old Wisconsin farm.

Believe me, yours, with all good wishes,

Take a little over one pint of rich, sweet milk, into which put two-thirds of a teacup of sugar and a little salt. Sift as much flour as you think will be required, into which mix four heaping teaspoonfuls of best baking powder. Stir into the milk and sugar six tablespoonfuls of very hot fresh lard, pour the mixture into the flour and make a sponge. When cooled sufficiently to prevent cooking the egg add one egg slightly beaten. Mix to a proper consistency, roll and cut into rings. It is hard to give a recipe where so much

MISS FRANCES E. WILLARD.

depends upon the judgment and care of the cook. Much depends upon having the lard in which the doughnuts are fried very hot before they are put in; otherwise they "soak up the fat" and are heavy.

Raised Doughnuts.

From Mrs. Ellen M. Chandler, of Vermont, Lady Manager.

One pint warmed milk, one cup sugar, one-half cup yeast, one-half teaspoon salt; mix about 10 A. M., let rise four hours then add: One cup sugar, two eggs, one-fourth cup lard, one-fourth cup butter. Knead and let rise in warm place until night, then roll thin and cut out; let rise over night in warm place and fry in the morning.

Ellen M. Chandler

Doughnuts.

From Mrs. Laura E. Howey, of Montana, Secretary State Board and Lady Manager.

Beat well together one egg, one cup sweet milk, one cup sugar (small cup), large teaspoonful of baking powder, sprinkle in two cups flour, piece butter size of an egg, pinch of salt. Knead soft, cook in skillet well filled with lard just to the boiling point; place in dripping pan, so that they may not get soggy with the grease while cooling off.

Laura E. Howey.

Doughnuts.

From Miss Annie M. Mahan, of West Virginia, Alternate Lady Manager.

One-half cup of butter, one cup of sour milk, one and one-half cup of sugar, four eggs, one teaspoon soda (in milk), nutmeg, flour to make it stiff enough to roll.

Callas.

A CREOLE CAKE EATEN HOT WITH COFFEE.

From Mrs. Belle H. Perkins, of Louisiana, President of State Board, Lady Manager.

One teacup of rice well boiled and mashed, one small coffee cup of sugar, two tablespoons yeast, three eggs and flour sufficient to make a thick batter; beat the whole well together and fry in hot lard. Be careful not to have the batter too thin, or it will not fry well.

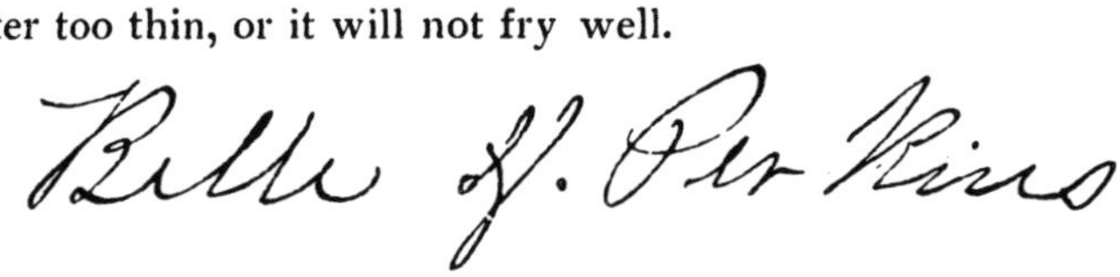

Apple Fritters.

From Mrs. M. P. Hart, of Ohio, President of State Board and Lady Manager.

Make a batter with one cup sweet milk, one teaspoonful sugar, two eggs, whites and yolks beaten separately, two cups flour, one teaspoonful baking powder mixed with flour Chop some good tart apples, mix them in the batter and fry in hot lard. Serve them with maple syrup.

Corn Fritters.

From Mrs. E. V. McConnell, of North Dakota, Lady Manager

Two eggs, one tablespoon of cream or sweet milk, one cup oyster crackers rolled fine, one can or six ears of sweet corn scraped from the cob, pepper and salt to taste. Put tablespoon butter in frying pan, have it hot and drop in batter by spoonfuls. Fry brown and serve hot for breakfast.

Clam Fritters.

From Mrs. Sallie S. Cotten, of North Carolina, President State Board and Alternate Lady Manager.

Open as oysters and chop fine. Make a stiff batter of eggs and flour, with a little black pepper. Stir into this batter the chopped clams and a little of the clam liquor, if necessary to make the batter the proper consistency. Fry in hot butter or lard.

White Corn Meal Cakes for Breakfast.

(A RHODE ISLAND DISH.)

From MRS. SARAH S. C. ANGELL, of Michigan, Lady Manager.

One pint white corn meal, into which you stir two saltspoonfuls salt. Gradually moisten this with boiling water until the mixture is somewhat thicker than hasty pudding. Stir constantly and after the right consistency is attained, beat thoroughly for two minutes. Drop from spoon into boiling lard and fry for five or six minutes. Serve immediately. It is of absolute importance that the water should be *boiling* and *kept so*, and therefore it is wise to bring the mixing dish very near the stove when the teakettle is heated. The same paste may be fried on a griddle like buckwheat cakes, but the first method makes the crispest, nuttiest flavor. This recipe makes bannocks enough for six people.

Sarah S. C. Angell

Corn Griddle Cakes or Old Virginia Slap Jacks.

From MISS LILY IRENE JACKSON, of West Virginia, Lady Manager.

One or two eggs, whites beaten to a froth; one quart of sweet milk; pinch of salt; meal enough to make a thin batter. Bake very thin on hot griddle and serve at once. Meal must not be too finely ground or bolted.

Lily Irene Jackson.

Fried Mush.

From Mrs. George Hoxworth, of Arizona, Alternate Lady Manager.

Three pints boiling water; one cup wheat flour; enough corn meal to make stiff batter. Fry while hot in plenty of grease. Think it more convenient than the old way and much better. A tablespoonful of sugar added makes it brown better

Mrs Geo Hoxworth

Superior Waffles.

From Mrs. Mary B. P. Black, of West Virginia, Alternate Lady Manager.

One quart of buttermilk; one pint of sweet new milk; four eggs, beaten separately; little salt; teaspoonful soda, dissolved in half teacup sour cream or buttermilk, and enough flour to make the dough of proper consistency. Sift your flour; begin with three pints, you may need less or more. Add buttermilk (sour cream will do instead), then sweet milk; then yolks of eggs, well beaten; then soda, having dissolved it in half teacupful of buttermilk or sour cream; add more flour now, should it be needed; lastly, whites of eggs, beaten to a stiff froth and stirred gently into the thin dough. Let the cook be care-

ful to fill the iron scantily half full, to bake, as these beautiful waffles to be crisp and tender must have ample space to rise.

Mary. B. P. Black

Mexican Enchiladas.

From Mrs. Franc Luse Albright, of New Mexico, Lady Manager.

1. To make the tortillas for the enchiladas, take one quart of blue corn meal mixed with water and salt, making a batter stiff enough to flatten out into round cakes, and bake on the bare hot lid.

2. To make the chili sauce: One cup of tepid water; three tablespoonfuls of ground chili; let boil down to a batter.

3. Filling for tortillas: Grated cheese and chopped onions, very fine.

Dip into a pan of boiling hot lard one tortilla; then dip this tortilla into the chili batter; then sprinkle with the filling, first the cheese and then the onion. Then put on one spoonful of chili batter and lay like a layer cake as many cakes as desired, and then pour over the chili batter. Cut like cake and serve hot.

Mrs Franc Luse Albright

PRESERVES

Tomato Conserve.

From MRS. CAROLINE E. DENNIS, of New York State, Alternate Lady Manager-at-Large.

Three pounds of sugar, to three pounds of tomatoes; add two lemons, peeled and sliced *very* thin; sliver the peel into smallest bits and add, with two inches of preserved ginger root, also cut very fine. Put tomatoes in a kettle, mash with a spoon, mix in the sugar, lemons and ginger, and boil slowly for *three* hours, or until the preserve is of the consistency of marmalade. This is a new and very choice sweetmeat; and, so far as we know, is not to be found in any other recipe-book.

Caroline E. Dennis.

Orange Marmalade.

From MRS. GOVERNOR OGLESBY, of Illinois, Lady Manager.

One dozen imperial oranges (good pulp and thick yellow skin); their scant weight in sugar. Peel six and grate the yellow rind without the white skin. Slice the peel from the other six into thin shreds; boil in three waters till very tender. Chop the oranges, removing all tough fibres and seeds; put on, with the juice that drains from the oranges, the sugar, a little water and the drained orange peel shreds; boil fifteen minutes, then add the pulp and grated rind and boil twenty minutes.

Emma Gillett Oglesby.

Compote of Apples.

From Mrs. Hattie E. Sladden, of Oregon, Alternate Lady Manager.

Make a syrup of one quart of water and one pint of white sugar. Pare and core (without breaking) six tart apples; stew in syrup until tender. Remove the apples to a deep glass dish; then add to the syrup a box of gelatine and cinnamon stick. When thoroughly dissolved, pour over the apples, first removing the cinnamon bark.

Hattie E. Sladden.

Steamed Peaches.

From Mrs. W. Newton Linch, of West Virginia, Lady Manager.

Place the fruit in a steamer and allow it to remain until skin can be removed, as that from a scalded tomato. Make a strong syrup of granulated sugar; place the peaches in the jar, pour the syrup over them very hot and seal at once. Steamed peaches make a delightful dish for lunch during

Emma Gillett Oglesby

their season. Do not make the syrup quite so strong and allow the peaches to get very cold before serving.

Isabel G. Linch

Quince Preserves.

From Mrs. M. P. Hart, of Ohio, President of State Board and Lady Manager.

Pare and core the quinces. Put the parings and cores into a kettle with sufficient water to cover them, and let them boil for a short time. Then strain and pour the liquid over the quinces. Let the quinces cook until they are soft before adding the sugar. The quinces and syrup must be boiled until they become transparent and of a rich color. The rule is one pound of sugar to a pound of fruit; a less quantity of sugar will be sufficient if the fruit should be well cooked and carefully sealed.

Mrs. M. P. Hart.

Watermelon Preserves.

From Mrs. H. K. Ingram, of Florida, Alternate Lady Manager.

Take a thick rind of a ripe watermelon. Cut into small strips, or any desirable fancy shapes; cut off all the red inside part and scrape off all the hard outside shell. Boil the pieces in water with peach or grape leaves and soda, in the proportion of a dozen leaves and a teaspoonful of soda to two quarts of water. When tender, take them out of the water and put them in cold water that has had half a large spoonful of alum dissolved in it. They will then become brittle and green. Let them soak in the alum water for an hour; then rinse in clear, cold water, and boil in a syrup made of equal weight of white sugar. Boil with them lemons cut in thin slices, allowing one lemon to two pounds of rind. Boil fifteen or twenty minutes. When a little cool, add a little essence of ginger, or if not the essence, boil in the syrup with the rinds a little green or ground ginger tied in bits of thin cloth. After three or four days pour the syrup off and boil down to a rich syrup that will just cover the rinds, and pour it over them scalding hot.

Mrs. H. H. Ingram.

Blackberry Jam.

From MRS. MARY S. MCNEAL, of Oklahoma, Alternate Lady Manager.

Put the fruit into a preserving kettle and boil fifteen or twenty minutes, stirring often and skimming off any scum that may rise; then add sugar in the proportion of three-fourths pound of sugar to one pound of fruit. Boil thirty minutes longer, stirring continually; when done, pour into small jars or jelly glasses.

Mary S. McNeal.

Canned Spiced Blackberries.

From MRS. H. J. PETO, of Arizona, Alternate Lady Manager

Wash the berries carefully and drain in a colander. For each quart of fruit add two cups granulated sugar and one-half cup of pure cider vinegar. Put all in a porcelain lined sauce pan, set on the stove and scald thoroughly; then add one-half dozen cloves and one and one-half ounces stick cinnamon for each quart of berries. While the fruit is hot, pour into glass jars and cover at once; it will be ready for use in three or four days. A delicious relish.

Mrs. H. J. Peto

Spiced Green Grapes.

From Mrs. George A. Mumford, of Rhode Island, Alternate Lady Manager.

Five pounds green grapes (wild are best); three pounds sugar; one pound raisins; one-half pint vinegar; one tablespoonful ground cloves; one tablespoonful ground allspice; one tablespoonful ground cinnamon. Stone the grapes and raisins; simmer one hour.

Mrs George A. Mumford

Orange Jelly.

From Mrs. Theresa J. Cochran, of Vermont, Alternate Lady Manager.

Grate the yellow rinds of two oranges and two lemons and squeeze the juice into a porcelain lined preserving kettle, adding the juice of two more oranges and removing all the seeds; put in the grated rind a quarter of a pound of sugar, or more if the fruit is sour, and a gill of water, and boil these ingredients together until a rich syrup is formed; meantime dissolve two ounces of gelatine in a quart of warm water, stirring it over the fire until it is entirely dissolved; then add the syrup, strain the jelly, and cool it in molds wet in cold water.—*White House Cook Book.*

Theresa J Cochran

Currant Jelly.

From Mrs. M. P. H. Beeson, of Oklahoma, Lady Manager.

One-half cup sugar to one cup currant juice. Boil for fifteen minutes. This will make a lovely jelly.

Mrs. M. P. H. Beeson

Crab Apple Jelly.

From Mrs. Genevieve M. Guthrie, of Oklahoma, Lady Manager.

Wash and quarter large Siberian crabs, but do not core; cover to the depth of an inch or two with cold water and cook to a mush; pour into a coarse cotton bag or strainer, and, when cool enough, press or squeeze hard to extract all of the juice. Take a piece of fine Swiss muslin or crinoline, wring out of water, spread over colander placed over a crock, and with a cup dip the juice slowly in, allowing plenty of time to run through; repeat this process twice, rinsing the muslin frequently. Allow the strained juice of four lemons to a peck of apples and three-quarters of a pound of sugar to each pint of juice. Boil the juice from ten to twenty minutes; while boiling, sift in the sugar slowly, stirring constantly, and boil five minutes longer. This is generally sufficient, but it is always safer to "try it" and ascertain whether it will jelly. This will make a clear, sparkling jelly.—*From Practical Housekeeping Cook Book.*

The jelly is excellent.

Mrs Genevieve M Guthrie

Pickled Onions.

From Mrs. Harriet A. Lucas, of Pennsylvania, Lady Manager

Peel carefully, by scalding, small onions; drain; place in salt and water, not too strong, for forty-eight hours; then drain again till dry. Put together one-half pint of milk and one-half pint water; place the small onions in it and allow them to scald, *not* boil; or they will be softened. Remove, rinse in cold water and drain. Place in a jar and pour over them white wine vinegar, with a little mace and small red peppers; no dark spice. You will have a beautifully white, mild pickled onion if this is carried out.

Oil Pickles.

From Mrs. Ida M. Ball, of Delaware, Lady Manager.

Two dozen large cucumbers, sliced without paring; sprinkle with salt; place in a colander to drain for two or three hours. One dozen onions prepared in the same way, separately. Put in a stone jar, in alternate layers, sprinkling between with ground black pepper and a mixture of mustard and oil, the mixture to be made in the proportion of a small box of mustard to one-half pint of salad oil. When the jar is full, pour in enough cold vinegar to cover.

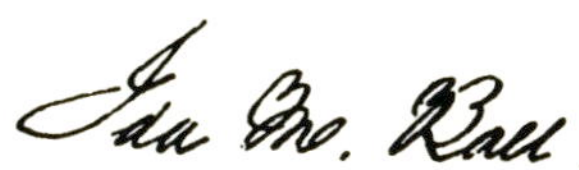

Mixed Pickles.

From MRS. SAM. S. FIFIELD, of Wisconsin, Lady Manager.

Take small cucumbers, onions, beans, cauliflower, broken up, and pour over boiling hot brine made of one teacup of coarse salt to a gallon of water, for three mornings. The fourth morning drain well. (I put into a flour sack and hang out doors until dry.) To one gallon of good cider vinegar put a teaspoon of pulverized alum, four of white mustard seed, two of celery seed, five or six tiny red peppers, a handful of cloves and as much of stick cinnamon; pour over the pickles when real hot; add a good quantity of horseradish root to keep pickles from moulding.

Cucumber Pickles.

From MRS. PARTHENIA P. RUE, of California, Lady Manager.

For two gallons of pickles, place the cucumbers in salt and water for three days; then rinse in fresh water. One teacupful of whole white mustard; one handful of whole cloves; allspice and black pepper; a teacupful of broken cinnamon. Put all into a large thin bag and boil in one quart vinegar. Put two or three red pepper pods and a few sprigs of horseradish root among the cucumbers, in a keg or jar. Take sufficient vinegar to cover them and put into it one pound of brown sugar; let it scald and cool a little; then pour over the pickles; then the spices and vinegar, allowing the spices to remain on top. The spices and vinegar must be poured off and scalded for five mornings, and, when cool, poured over the pickles; the last day pour over a cup of molasses. Use good cider vinegar. If desired sweeter, sugar to vinegar when heating. Cucumbers used late in the season make better pickles than the earlier ones. Put cucumbers in salt water when freshly picked.

Parthenia P. Rue.

Green Cucumber Pickle.

From Mrs. Cora Payne Jackson, of Kentucky, Lady Manager.

One gallon of cider vinegar; one pound of brown sugar; one tablespoon of allspice; one tablespoon of cloves; one tablespoon of black pepper; one tablespoon of mace; two tablespoons of root ginger; two tablespoons of celery; two tablespoons of white mustard; one handful of horseradish. After it begins to boil add cold cucumbers, well soaked, and boil until tender enough to pierce with a fork.

Cora Payne Jackson

Ripe Cucumber Pickle.

From Miss Mary Elliott McCandless, of Pennsylvania, Lady Manager.

Slice twenty-five large cucumbers in pieces between one and two inches thick; lay in salt water two days; wash out the salt. Boil in alum water half an hour, alum size of a walnut (English); take out and boil in ginger water an hour; one ounce of ginger and water to cover. Make a syrup of five pounds of light brown sugar, three quarts of vinegar, one pint of water, two ounces of whole cloves, two ounces of stick cinnamon, half an ounce of whole allspice, half an ounce of mace (put spices in bags). Let all boil until a rich syrup, then put in the cucumbers and boil between one and two hours.

Mary Elliott McCandless

Gooseberry Catsup.

From Mrs. Amey M. Starkweather, of Rhode Island, Superintendent State Work and Lady Manager.

Nine pounds of gooseberries; add five pounds of sugar, one quart of vinegar, three tablespoonfuls of cinnamon, one and one-half each of allspice and cloves. The gooseberries should be nearly or quite ripe. Take off the blossoms, wash, and put them into a porcelain kettle, scald, then put through a colander, add the sugar and spices; boil fifteen minutes; then add the vinegar; bottle immediately before it cools. Almost any recipe for spiced gooseberries makes a good recipe when the gooseberries are put through a colander or coarse sieve, and the vinegar added, cooled in this way.

If you wish a smaller recipe, use the following: To

four quarts of fruit, take three pounds of sugar, one pint of vinegar, one tablespoonful each of ground cloves, allspice and cinnamon. Make as in the above recipe.

Cabbage Pickle.

From MRS. CARRINGTON MASON, of Tennessee, Alternate Lady Manager.

Quarter small, hard heads of cabbage, removing the outer leaves; put in a brine for three days, then let it soak in fresh water six hours. Wipe perfectly dry, squeezing the water out. Scald the cabbage in weak vinegar and water, to which add turmeric in a thin muslin bag. Then put into a stone jar alternate layers of cabbage and seasoning as follows: Mace, ginger, cinnamon, white mustard seeds, onions, red pepper, and horse radish. Bring to a boil enough good cider vinegar to cover the whole, and pour into the jar hot.

Picalilly.

From MRS. ELLA RAY MILLER, of Idaho, Alternate Lady Manager.

One peck green tomatoes; twelve large onions; one ounce each of allspice, cloves, cinnamon, whole pepper and white mustard seed; two ounces flour of mustard, one and one-half pound sugar. Slice and salt tomatoes, drain over night. Put spices in bags, cover all with vinegar, and boil till tender. Seal in glass jars.

Sweet Pickled Peaches.

From Mrs. Nellie B. Plumer, of Pennsylvania, Alternate Lady Manager.

Ten pounds peaches—pared; five pounds sugar; one quart best cider vinegar; one tablespoonful allspice; one tablespoonful mace; one tablespoonful cinnamon; one teaspoonful cloves. Put the spices in thin muslin bags. Boil all together half hour; then put in the peaches, and boil twenty minutes. Take out the fruit with a skimmer, and spread upon dishes to cool. Boil the syrup until thick, pack the peaches in glass jars, and pour syrup over them scalding hot.

Chow-Chow Pickles.

From Mrs. H. K. Ingram, of Florida, Alternate Lady Manager.

One-half peck green tomatoes; one dozen peppers; two heads cabbage (medium size); one-half peck onions; one-fourth peck cucumbers. Chop fine (or, better still, run through a sausage grinder), and mix thoroughly with three handfuls of salt. Pour all into a thin bag to drain for twelve hours, or over night. At the end of this time put sufficient vinegar to cover into a large iron, tin or porcelain vessel, and add two ounces black pepper grains, two ounces allspice grains, two ounces celery seed, one-fourth pound mustard, one pound sugar. Scald the vinegar and pour contents of bag into it; add the spices, mix well, and let all come to a boil, and remove instantly. This will be found equal to the best imported bottled chow-chow.

Mrs. H. H. Ingram.

Mustard Chow-Chow.

From Mrs. Alice B. Castleman, of Kentucky, Alternate Lady Manager.

Two dozen cucumbers, cut in chunks about an inch thick; two heads of cabbage, chopped fine. Sprinkle with salt and let stand all night. One dozen large green peppers, chopped up; five dozen small seed onions. Soak the onions and peppers separately in salt water all night; next morning squeeze all the salt water from them. Then place in a kettle a layer of pickle and a layer of seasoning composed of two ounces of white mustard seed; two ounces celery seed; one ounce turmeric; one-half pound box of Coleman's mustard, mixed smooth with vinegar, adding two and one-half pounds brown sugar. After putting all in the kettle, cover with vinegar and boil thirty minutes. This recipe makes two gallons of pickles, and one and one half gallons of vinegar covers it. Use best cider vinegar.

Alice B Castleman

Chow-Chow.

From Miss Mary Elliott McCandless, of Pennsylvania, Lady Manager.

One peck green tomatoes; two large heads of cabbage; two good sized onions; three small red peppers; one-fourth pound yellow mustard seed; one-fourth pound ground mustard; one and one-half ounces celery seed; one tablespoonful cayenne pepper, three quarts best vinegar; one quart granulated sugar. Slice tomatoes, salt them, then chop very fine, and drain all green water off; put the chopped tomatoes on in a preserving kettle, with some good vinegar, bring them to the scald, then pour in colander to drain and cool. Chop cabbage, onions and peppers fine, and *when the tomatoes are cold*, mix all together. Bring to boil vinegar, sugar, mustard seed, celery seed, red pepper and more salt. Mix ground mustard with chopped tomatoes, cabbage, etc. When the vinegar, sugar, etc., is cold, pour on the chopped mixture; stir thoroughly and put in wide-mouthed bottles.

Mary Elliott McCandless

Cheese Fonda.

From Miss Hattie T. Hundley, of Alabama, Lady Manager.

One cup of bread crumbs, very dry and fine; two scant cups of milk; one-half pound of old cheese, grated; three eggs, whipped very light, and one tablespoonful of butter. Season with pepper and salt and a pinch of soda dissolved in hot water and stirred into the milk. Soak the crumbs in the milk, beat with these the eggs, butter, seasoning, and lastly the cheese; put into a buttered baking dish, put dry bread crumbs on top and bake in a rather quick oven until a delicate brown. Serve immediately.—*Mrs. Henderson's Cook Book.*

Hattie T. Hundley.

Cheese Sticks.

From Mrs. Margaret M. Ratcliffe, of Arkansas, Alternate Lady Manager.

Six tablespoons of grated cheese; two tablespoons of melted butter; enough flour to make a soft dough. Roll thin, cut in strips and bake in floured pan in quick oven.

Margaret M. Ratcliffe

Lemon Pie.

From MRS. L. M. N. STEVENS, of Maine, Lady Manager.

One cup sugar; juice of one lemon; one egg and yolks of two eggs; one dessertspoonful rolled cracker, scalded in two-thirds cup milk. Bake in a deep plate. After baking frost with the whites of two eggs beaten stiff, adding two spoonfuls of sugar. Brown the frosting a little.

Ideal Lemon Pie.

From MRS. IDA L. TURNER, of Texas, Lady Manager.

Make the crust, line pie tin and bake. While it is baking prepare the following filling: Grate one lemon (do not roll it); after the yellow rind is all grated, squeeze in the juice and if any little cells go in, do not say them nay; then put in a cupful of sugar and the yolks of two eggs; stir well together; upon this pour a large cupful of cold water, into which has been stirred a dessertspoonful of corn starch; put all into a sauce pan and stir until it is cooked into a rich, clear, straw-colored jelly. Then fill the crust and from the whites of the eggs make a meringue to cover each. Put into the oven for one brief instant.

Lemon Pie.

From Mrs. Virginia C. Meredith, of Indiana, Lady Manager and Vice-Chairman of Executive Committee.

Two cups of sugar; one cup of boiling water; four eggs; two lemons; one and one-half tablespoon flour. Stir the sugar and flour well together; add the juice and grated rind of the lemons; to this add the well beaten yolks; after stirring well, add the boiling water; put over a clear fire and stir constantly until it boils, then pour into the shells. Spread over the top a meringue made of the whites of the four eggs and one tablespoon of sugar; place in the oven and brown slightly. This is sufficient for two pies. The shells should be made of ordinary pie pastry and baked before being filled with the mixture.

Isabel Somerset

LADY HENRY SOMERSET, MEMBER OF THE BRITISH WOMEN'S COMMITTEE FOR THE WORLD'S COLUMBIAN EXPOSITION.

Lemon Pie.

From Miss Lucia B. Perea, of New Mexico, Alternate Lady Manager.

One and one-half cups of sugar; one cup of water; two tablespoonfuls flour or corn starch; one tablespoonful butter; yolks of three eggs; two lemons, grated; add juice, beat well all together, then boil until thick. Beat up one cup of pulverized sugar with the whites of three eggs. Pour over the pie when done, and brown.

Pumpkin Pie.

From Mrs. Frances C. Holley, of North Dakota, Alternate Lady Manager.

Pare pumpkin, cut into inch pieces; steam till well done, or stew until soft and dry; then sift through a wire sieve or colander. Add one well beaten egg for each pie, also one tablespoonful of cream, if you have it, for each, together with sufficient milk to give the required thickness when cooked. Sugar and salt to your taste, flavor with nutmeg, adding also a little ginger. Use deep custard plates; bake, rather slowly at first, until well thickened and nicely brown on top.

Apple Custard Pie.

From Mrs. Annie L. Y. Orff, of Missouri, Alternate Lady Manager.

One cup milk; yolks of two eggs; four grated apples; small spoon of melted butter; one-half cup sugar; nutmeg to flavor; pinch of salt. Bake in one crust. Make a frosting with whites of eggs and two spoons of sugar. Brown delicately.

Annie L. Y. Orff

Cream Pie.

From Mrs. M. R. Lee, of Mississippi, Lady Manager.

Put one-half pint milk and one-half cupful sugar in a frying pan and let it come to a boil; then dissolve one tablespoonful corn starch in a little milk reserved from the half pint. Add to it the beaten yolk of one egg, stir into the boiling milk, and when thickened and smooth, remove and add a little salt and lemon flavoring. Pour into a flaky crust that has been just baked, and frost with the white of one egg and one tablespoonful sugar; place in hot stove till a delicate brown.

M. R. Lee

Cream Pie

From Mrs. Louise Campbell, of New Mexico, Alternate Lady Manager.

Bake an undercrust. Boil one pint of sweet milk; when boiling, stir in one-quarter cup of corn starch, one-half a cup of sugar, and the yolks of two eggs, which must be well beaten together. Cook thoroughly, flavor with vanilla, and add a little salt. Pour this mixture into the baked crust. Beat the whites of the two eggs, and to them add half a cup of sugar, and use as meringue.

Louise Campbell

Apple Pie.

From Mrs. Alice Vineyard Brown, of North Dakota, Alternate Lady Manager.

Sift into a chopping bowl three small cups of flour; then with the knife chop in thoroughly one cup of lard, one-half cup of butter, that have been on ice for an hour; mix with four to six tablespoons of ice water, as may be needed to handle, roll thin and line a shell, into which slice thinly any tart apples that will cook rather quickly. Dredge with the grated rind of a lemon — a somewhat dry lemon is preferable — which has been mixed thoroughly with one tablespoon of sugar and one small teaspoon of corn starch. Now break an egg into a bowl, beat well and add four tablespoons of sugar and one cup of rich milk; pour this over the apples; with the jag iron cut the remainder of the paste into narrow strips and lay across to form squares. Bake in a moderate oven until the custard "sets." Place on ice in summer; eat slightly warm in winter.

Alice Vineyard Brown.

Pie Crust.

From MRS. ANNIE L. Y. ORFF, of Missouri, Alternate Lady Manager.

One cup lard; one-half cup cold water; a pinch of salt, and flour enough to roll. This will make exactly two pies.

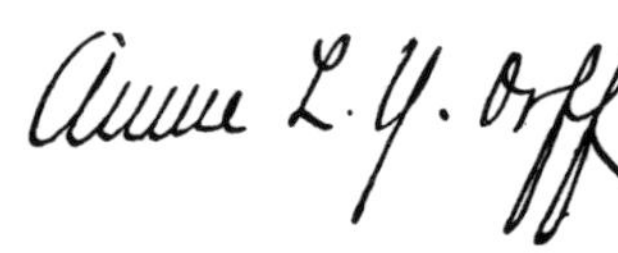

Mince Meat.

From MRS. MARCIA LOUISE GOULD, of Illinois, President State Board and Lady Manager.

Two pounds of lean fresh beef boiled; when cold chop fine; one pound of beef suet cleared of strings and minced to a powder; five pounds of apples, pared and chopped; two pounds of raisins, seeded and chopped; one pound of Sultana raisins, washed and picked over; two pounds of currants, washed and *carefully* picked over; three-quarters of a pound of citron, chopped fine; two tablespoonfuls of cinnamon, one of nutmeg (powdered), two of mace, one of cloves, one of allspice, one of fine salt; two and a quarter pounds of brown sugar; one quart brown sherry, and one pint best brandy or three pints of grape juice.

Mince Meat.

From MRS. LAURA P. COLEMAN, of Colorado, Lady Manager.

Two pounds of beef; half pound suet; half pound butter; five pounds apples; two pounds raisins; two pounds seedless raisins; half pound citron; three tablespoonfuls cinnamon, two of mace, two of allspice; one nutmeg; three pounds brown sugar; half gallon sweet cider. Boil beef until tender, then chop fine; also chop suet, apples and citron. Then mix all the ingredients thoroughly and boil until the apples are cooked. After removing from the stove add one-half teacupful of brandy if desired.

Laura P. Coleman

PUDDING

Graham Christmas Pudding.

From MRS. ROLLIN A. EDGERTON, of Arkansas, Secretary of State Board and Lady Manager.

The Christmas pudding which I add was served up this Christmas on my table and pronounced delicious. Dyspeptics need not fear this "Plum Pudding," and it is rich enough to please the most fastidious.

Wishing your philanthropic efforts every success, I am,

Very truly yours,

Mrs Rollin A. Edgerton

Beat two eggs; take one-half cup of sweet milk; one-half cup of molasses, in which dissolve one-half teaspoon of soda; a lump of butter the size of an egg; one cup of Graham flour (don't sift); two cups of flour, in which a cup of stoned raisins are well rubbed; one small teaspoon of salt; spice with cinnamon, cloves and nutmeg, one teaspoonful all together. Then steam two hours and serve with a hard sauce of butter and fine sugar creamed together, with one well beaten egg and grated nutmeg as a finish. Wholesome, delicious, and extremely simple to prepare.

Graham Pudding.

From Mrs. George A. Mumford, of Rhode Island, Alternate Lady Manager.

One and one-half cups of Graham flour; one cup of milk; one-half cup of molasses; one cup of raisins, seeded and chopped; one teaspoonful soda; one-half teaspoonful salt. Sift the Graham flour to make it light, but return the bran. Dissolve the soda in one tablespoonful of the milk and add the remainder of the milk, molasses and salt. Then pour all the mixture on the Graham flour, beating it thoroughly with a spoon; then stir in the fruit (and spice if you wish). Pour the pudding into a well greased mould and steam four hours. Serve with a wine or any rich sauce.

Mrs George A. Mumford

Lady Ross Fig Pudding.

From Mrs. Wm. P. Lynde, of Wisconsin, Lady Manager.

Three-quarters pound grated bread; one-half pound best figs, minced fine; six ounces minced beef suet; six ounces sugar; one teacup sweet milk; a little nutmeg; one egg. Mix the bread and suet together; then add figs, sugar and nutmeg; then the egg, well beaten; lastly the milk. Boil in a mould four hours.

Wine Sauce—Two cups sugar; one-half cup butter. Stir to a cream; then add one glass of wine and some flavoring and a little nutmeg; then pour in a small cup boiling water and set on the stove in a pan or kettle of water and keep hot until served.

Mrs. Wm P. Lynde

Alexandre Pudding.

From Mrs. M. D. Thatcher, of Colorado, Lady Manager.

Set a jelly mould on ice; put a layer of maraschino jelly (or any wine jelly) in the bottom of the mould; when set, add a layer of pink jelly (made by adding a drop of prepared cochineal); when set, put a lining in the centre of the mould; if you have not the centre-form, use a small tin baking-powder box, placing it in the centre of the mould; then add alternate layers of the jellies until the mould is filled, and when well set and firm, gently withdraw the lining (or can), filling the hollow thus formed with a custard cream. When all is quite firm, turn out on a dish and serve with whipped cream around the pudding.

Mrs. M. D. Thatcher

Plum Pudding.

From Mrs. Florence H. Kidder, of North Carolina, Lady Manager.

One and one-half pounds of stoned raisins, torn in half; one pound of currants; one and one-half pounds of citron, cut fine; one and one-quarter pounds of butter; one pound of sugar; eight eggs, well beaten; one pound of stale bread crumbs; one and one-half pints of sweet milk, boiled and poured on bread crumbs; two grated nutmegs; two tablespoons of cinnamon; one tablespoon of mace, one of cloves and two of allspice; eight tablespoons of sifted flour, rubbed in with fruit; one-half pint of French brandy and one-half pint of Madeira or sherry. Have a bag two thicknesses of white unbleached cloth; grease and flour the inside well;

pour in mixture, tie tightly to exclude water, and leave room for pudding to swell. Put in a pot of boiling water, which must be kept boiling for five hours. Put plate in bottom of pot to prevent sticking. The bag must be turned repeatedly and kept under water.

Sauce for Plum Pudding—Butter and powdered sugar, thoroughly stirred, and seasoned with wine and nutmeg. When pudding is ready to serve, pour alcohol over it and set on fire.

This recipe makes a large pudding, but it can be packed away with brandy poured over it, and can be used by steaming over as long as it lasts.

English Plum Pudding.

From MRS. PHŒBE M. HARTPENCE, of Ohio, Chairman Committee on Woman's Work, Lady Manager.

One cup molasses; one cup sour milk; one cup suet, chopped fine; one cup raisins; one-half cup currants; two and one-half cups flour; one teaspoonful soda. Mix well, salt and spice to taste, and steam two hours.

Dressing—Mix one heaping tablespoonful flour and two of sugar; add to these grated nutmeg. Stir and add one-half pint of boiling water; add to this a small tablespoonful of butter, a little lemon and vanilla, one teaspoonful vinegar. Let it come to a boil, and if too thick, add more water.

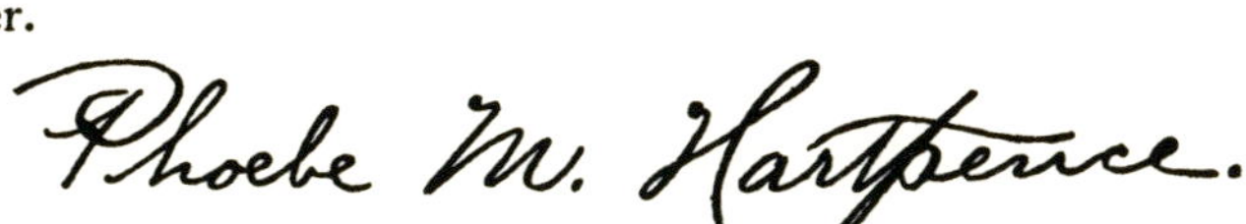

English Plum Pudding.

From Mrs. S. W. McLaughlin, of North Dakota, Lady Manager.

A pound of suet, chopped fine; a pint of sugar; one pound of grated stale bread; one pound of raisins, two of currants; a glass of unfermented wine or jelly; two teaspoonfuls of ginger, one of soda; two nutmegs; half a pint of milk; a little salt. Beat well and steam five hours. Serve with rich sauce.

Vegetable Plum Pudding.

From Miss Mary E. Busselle, of New Jersey, Lady Manager.

One-half pound flour; one-half pound chopped suet; one-half pound currants; one-half pound prunes; one-quarter pound grated raw carrots; three-quarters pound grated raw potatoes; one-half pound brown sugar; one large teaspoonful of baking powder; pinch of salt. Flavor with a teaspoonful each of nutmeg, cinnamon and cloves. The moisture from the raw vegetables makes sufficient wetting.

Plum Pudding.

From Mrs. Helen C. Brayton, of South Carolina, Vice-President of State Board and Lady Manager.

One pound seedless raisins; one pound dried currants; one pound stale bread crumbs; one-half pound finely

MRS. CLARA L. McADOW.

chopped beef suet; one-fourth pound shredded citron; eight eggs; one quart milk; one-half cup sugar; mace or nutmeg; one gill of brandy; one teaspoon salt; eggs well beaten and put in last; raisins floured before stirring in. Boil gently five hours without stopping. Water must be boiling when pudding is put in and kept boiling till done. Eat with liquid wine sauce. Pour alcohol around pudding and set it on fire. A sprig of holly in centre for Christmas.

Helen C Brayton

Christmas Plum Pudding.

From Mrs. Alice J. Whalen, of Utah, Lady Manager.

One pint and a half of grated bread crumbs (soft, not dried), one pint of chopped suet, one pint of currants, one pint and a half of stoned raisins, half a cup of citron shaved thin, one scant cup of sugar, half a teaspoonful of salt, half a teaspoonful of grated nutmeg, one teaspoonful of mace, five eggs, yolks and whites beaten separately, two even teaspoonfuls of flour made into a thin batter with milk, and half a glass of brandy; mix in the order given and steam four hours.

Sauce for Pudding — Cream one-fourth pound butter, add one-fourth pound of brown sugar and stir over hot water until liquid, then add the yolks of two eggs, well beaten; stir until it thickens. Just before serving add a cup of brandy and hot water equal parts.

Alice J. Whalen

Cherry Pudding.

From MRS. LOUISE L. BARTON, of Idaho, Alternate Lady Manager.

One pint of flour, one heaping teaspoonful of baking powder, lump of butter the size of a hickory nut, one pinch of salt, wet up with milk to a thick batter as stiff as for gems; add one pint of cherries with the juice strained off; stir the cherries into the batter; steam in stem cake dish; butter cake dish, and steam three-quarters of an hour. When done turn out on plate.

Sauce for same—One cup of cherry juice, one cup of sugar, one cup of water, small lump of butter, one tablespoonful of thickening; when it boils up add two tablespoons of cherry wine and nutmeg to taste. This pudding is enough for twelve persons.

Louise L. Barton

Bread and Butter Pudding.

From MRS. NANCY HUSTON BANKS, of Kentucky, Alternate Lady Manager-at-Large.

Butter thin slices of bread and place them in dish; then a layer of fruit, such as berries (or preserves will do); then another layer of bread and butter, and so on until the dish is full. Then pour beaten eggs in a quart of milk, say three eggs to the quart, over the ingredients and bake half an hour.

Nancy Huston Banks

Delicate Indian Pudding.

From Mrs. S. W. McLaughlin, of North Dakota, Lady Manager.

One quart of milk, two heaping tablespoonfuls of Indian meal, four of sugar, one of butter, three eggs, one teaspoonful of salt; boil the milk in the double boiler; sprinkle the meal into it, stirring all the while; cook twelve minutes, stirring often. Beat together the eggs, salt, sugar and half a teaspoonful of ginger; stir the butter into the meal and milk; pour this gradually on the egg mixture. Bake slowly one hour.

Baked Indian Pudding.

From Mrs. Mariam D. Cooper, of Montana, Alternate Lady Manager.

Three large tablespoons corn meal. Scald one quart sweet milk; stir meal in while hot; small lump butter, one cup molasses, salt; add one pint cold milk after putting in pan; bake five hours; eat with a little butter.

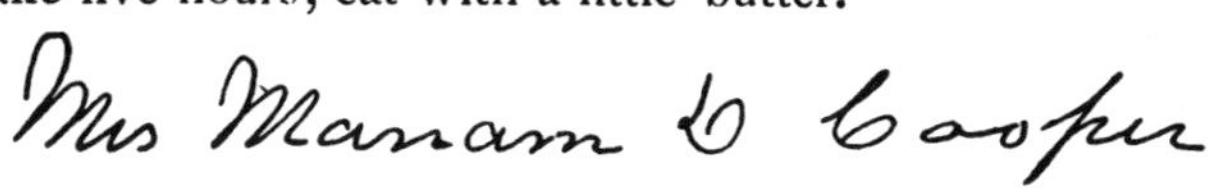

Prune Roll.

From Mrs. Clark Waring, of South Carolina, Alternate Lady Manager.

Soak two pounds of prunes in cold water over night; drain through a colander and seed them. Make your puff paste; roll it out; place your prunes on the paste, sprinkling with a little sugar on top; then roll smoothly. Bake in a steady heat and serve hot with hard butter sauce, or very rich wine sauce.

Mrs Clark Waring

Prune Pudding.

From Mrs. Hattie E. Sladden, of Oregon, Alternate Lady Manager.

Thoroughly wash one pound of prunes; soak over night, stewing in same water until very soft; sweeten to the taste while cooking. Next mash the fruit, removing the stones, and add half a box of gelatine (previously dissolved in a little water) and whites of four eggs well beaten. Serve cold with cream.

Hattie E. Sladden.

Prune Pudding.

From Mrs. Mary S. McNeal, of Oklahoma, Alternate Lady Manager.

To a large cup of stewed prunes (chopped fine) add a large tablespoon of sugar and a pinch of cream of tartar; then the well beaten whites of seven eggs. Bake about twenty minutes in a shallow pan or dish with a greased paper in bottom so pudding can be turned out without breaking. Serve cold with whipped cream.

Mary S. McNeal.

Prune Pudding.

From MRS. JOHN R. WILSON, of South Dakota, Lady Manager.

One cup of prunes, one cup of raisins, one cup suet, one cup molasses, one cup bread crumbs, one - half cup milk, one and one - half cup flour, one teaspoon soda, one teaspoon each of cloves and cinnamon, one - half nutmeg. Steam three hours.

Bread Pudding.

From MRS. KATE CANTHON McDANIEL, of Texas, Alternate Lady Manager.

Place in a buttered tin alternate layers of buttered bread and raisins or chopped apples. Take the yolks of four eggs and two cups of sugar, beat until light; add a pint of sweet milk; flavor to suit taste; pour over the bread and bake in a moderate oven. When done, beat the whites to a stiff froth, add a little sugar, flavor, heap on the pudding and return to the oven until a light brown.

Chocolate Pudding.

From MISS MARY B. HANCOCK, of Iowa, Treasurer State Board and Alternate Lady Manager.

One quart milk, heated in double kettle; six tablespoons of grated chocolate; four yolks of eggs, beaten well and mixed with eight tablespoons of sugar; two tablespoons, or a little more, of cornstarch, dissolved in a little cold milk.

Let these ingredients just come to a boil and flavor with vanilla, place in pudding dish and cover on top with the stiff froth of four whites of eggs, sweetened with three large teaspoons of sugar, into which stick twenty-four separated blanched almonds. To be eaten with sweetened cream flavored with a little vanilla.

Danish Pudding.

Ten eggs; one quart of cream; eight tablespoonfuls of sugar; one dessertspoon of vanilla. Beat the eggs and sugar together, heat the cream and pour over it.

Caramel— Two and one-half cups of brown sugar, cooked until very brown; then add one cup of cold water and pour into the pudding and bake.

Mary B. Hancock

Delicious Pudding.

From Mrs. Elizabeth C. Langworthy, of Nebraska, Lady Manager.

To two cups of boiling milk add four tablespoons of flour and two of butter, beaten together. When thickened, add four tablespoons sugar and yolks of eight eggs. When quite cold add whites of eggs, well beaten, and bake in moderate oven twenty minutes. Serve hot with sauce made of one-half cup of butter, beaten to a cream, one cup of sugar, added gradually; white of egg, beaten stiff. Add lemon or vanilla to taste.

Elizabeth C. Langworthy

MRS. HELEN M. BARKER.

Suet Pudding.

From Mrs. Helen M. Barker, of South Dakota, Lady Manager.

One cup chopped suet; one cup molasses (New Orleans); one cup chopped raisins; one cup sweet milk; three cups sifted flour; one teaspoon soda dissolved in milk; spices to taste. Steam three hours.

Serve with sauce made as follows: One cup of sugar; one-half cup of butter; one egg—cream well. Cook by pouring boiling water and stirring constantly.

Suet Pudding.

From Mrs. Leander Stone, of Chicago, Lady Manager.

The following recipe for Suet Pudding has been unfailing in my family for forty years past. Sincerely yours,

One cup molasses; one cup suet, chopped fine; one cup sweet milk; one cup fruit; one teaspoon salt; a piece of soda size of a pea; flour to make it as stiff as pound cake. Steam three hours.

Queen Pudding.

From Mrs. L. C. Gillespie, of Tennessee, Lady Manager.

One quart of sweet milk; one pint of grated bread crumbs; one teacup of white sugar; four eggs, and butter the size of hen's egg. Beat yolks of eggs with the sugar until very light; cream butter and add to eggs and sugar; then stir in bread crumbs and after these ingredients are well mixed, pour in the milk, stirring all thoroughly. Bake in porcelain pan or granite iron, under a good fire with a well heated oven. Twenty minutes is sufficient time to bake it. You do not want it baked until it is stiff and hard, but it must quake as you lift it from the oven. You now cover the top of the pudding, first with a half glass of jelly cut in very thin slices, and over this you put the whites of the four eggs, beaten to a stiff froth, to which you add and beat in two tablespoonfuls of sugar. Put the pudding again into the stove, this time in the top, where the whites of the eggs may brown quickly. Serve cold, with cream whipped and flavored with vanilla. This, properly baked, is a delicate, delicious pudding.

Mrs. L. C. Gillespie

Steam Pudding.

From Mrs. John S. Briggs, of Nebraska, Lady Manager.

One quart flour, one coffeecup chopped raisins or currants, one teacup chopped suet, one teacup half filled with molasses, finish with brown sugar, one teaspoon soda, two teacupfuls sweet milk, a little salt, mix and steam three hours.

Steam Pudding Sauce — Three-quarters of a cup of butter, one and a half cups of sugar, one egg, juice and grated rind of a lemon all well beaten together. Just before serving, pour on the beaten mixture one pint of boiling water.

Mrs. John S. Briggs

Steam Pudding.

From Mrs. Clara L. McAdow, of Montana, Lady Manager.

Four cups flour, four spoons baking powder, one-half can cherries, little salt, stir a stiff batter; steam one and a half hours.

Baked Huckleberry Pudding.

From Mrs. Nellie B. Plumer, of Pennsylvania, Alternate Lady Manager.

Two cups light brown sugar, one cup butter and lard mixed, one cup sour milk, four eggs, one teaspoonful of soda, one quart huckleberries. Make the dough as thick as jelly cake; bake three-quarters of an hour in a moderate oven. Use wine or butter sauce as preferred.

Minnie's Lemon Pudding.

From Mrs. H. J. Peto, of Arizona, Alternate Lady Manager.

Two lemons, two tablespoonfuls of cornstarch, one and one-half cup granulated sugar, three eggs. Grate rind of one lemon; squeeze juice and pulp of two lemons; beat yolks of the eggs with a portion of the sugar, then add balance of sugar and the grated rind and lemon juice; mix the cornstarch with a little water; add boiling water, stirring constantly until thick and clear; add the ingredients previously mixed and stir until thoroughly incorporated with the starch; pour into a pudding dish, cool a little, then set into the oven for a few minutes to brown; beat the whites of the eggs stiff; add a little powdered sugar and put over top of pudding; brown slightly. May be served warm, but is delicious if set on ice until thoroughly cold.

Mrs H. J. Peto

Cup Pudding.

From Mrs. Marie J. Gaston, of South Dakota, Alternate Lady Manager.

One-half cup of sugar, one cup flour, one-half cup cold water, one egg, one tablespoonful of butter, two level teaspoonfuls baking powder, a pinch of salt. Grease cups and put in the bottom of the cups a little fruit, such as dried currants, cherries, etc., or a little preserves; pour in the batter, filling the cups a little more than half full; set them in a steamer and steam forty minutes. This will make five cups. Served with the following sauce:

Pudding Sauce—Six tablespoonfuls pulverized sugar, two tablespoons of butter, one egg; beat altogether with an egg beater; flavor with vanilla. When ready to serve, add one cup of boiling water.

Marie J. Gaston

Italian Roll.

From Mrs. F. H. Daniell, of New Hampshire, Alternate Lady Manager.

Mix together one-half pound fine flour and from four to five ounces of sifted sugar; put in a sauce pan and bring to the boiling point, one-half pint of new milk and one-quarter pound fresh butter; stir in gradually the flour and sugar; beat well four fresh eggs, add them with the grated rind of a lemon, stirring until the mixture is thick like dough. Put it on a pasteboard and when cold roll to the desired thickness, about one-quarter of an inch thick; lay any kind of jam over the paste, roll it into a bolster-like form and bake. Serve cold, whole, or in slices nearly an inch thick. Time twenty to twenty-five minutes to bake.

Mrs Frank H. Daniell

Chaperone Pudding.

From Mrs. Annie L. Y. Orff, of Missouri, Alternate Lady Manager.

One pint nice, fine bread crumbs to one quart of milk; one cup sugar; yolks of four eggs beaten light; grated rind of one lemon; butter size of an egg; bake until done, but not watery. Whip the whites of four eggs beaten stiff; beat in a teacup of sugar; then add the juice of one lemon; pour over pudding; eat cold.

Annie L. Y. Orff

Apple Pudding.

From Mrs. Ida L. Turner, of Texas, Lady Manager.

Pare and core ten good sized apples. Stew them to a pulp, with sugar enough to sweeten; thickly butter the sides and bottom of an earthen baking dish and press all around them crumbs from the inside of a loaf of bread, having them nearly an inch thick. Mix with the apples a tablespoonful of butter and one egg, beaten; put the apples into the dish without disturbing the crumbs; over the surface put a layer of crumbs, dotted with bits of butter, and bake the pudding until brown; turn a platter over the pudding dish, quickly turn both upside down so the pudding will slip out on platter. Dust with powdered sugar and serve hot.

Mrs Ida L. Turner.

Baked Apple Dumpling.

From Mrs. Schuyler Colfax, of Indiana, Alternate Lady Manager-at-Large.

Pare and core tart apples; fill the centres with sugar, butter and a small pinch of cinnamon or a little grated nutmeg. Make a rich, light pie crust, roll, cut in squares, fold a square around each apple, put them into a buttered pan. Now cream together half a cup of butter and a cup of sugar, and put over the whole, when they are ready for the oven, pour a little cold water into the pan, and bake slowly an hour and a half or two hours.

Ellen W. Colfax

Foam Sauce.

From Mrs. Carrington Mason, of Tennessee, Alternate Lady Manager.

Three teacupfuls of pulverized sugar; one of butter; three tablespoonfuls of flour; one teacupful of boiling water. Beat butter, sugar and flour together thoroughly; stir into the boiling water; let it boil up and flavor with vanilla, and serve immediately.

Mrs. Carrington Mason

Sponge Cake.

From MRS. ISABELLA BEECHER HOOKER, of Connecticut, Lady Manager.

The recipe I send for Sponge Cake was one constantly in use twenty-five years ago, when this picture was taken, and so might well be used in connection with that recipe, which is the only one in which I feel a personal interest.

It gives me pleasure to oblige you, and I am cordially yours for womankind, also for mankind.

Isabella Beecher Hooker

Ten eggs; one-half pound flour; one pound pulverized sugar; one lemon; small teaspoon salt. Beat yolks separately and very thoroughly; add sugar, salt, lemon juice and grated peel, and beat again. Beat whites to stiffness and add to the yolks, beating well together. Then cut the flour in slowly with large knife and *avoid beating* after this. Bake in two deep, long, narrow tins, in rather slow oven, but hot on the bottom. The secret of success is in cutting in the flour and the baking. But few people will believe this and cannot reach my standard. I have made this cake for forty years with uniform success.

MRS. ISABELLA BEECHER HOOKER.

Sponge Cake.

From MRS. MARTHA A. GRIGGS, of Washington, Alternate Lady Manager.

Six eggs; two cups of sugar. Beat twenty minutes; stir in lightly two cups of flour and a little salt. Flavor to taste.

Sponge Cake.

From MRS. MARIE J. GASTON, of South Dakota, Alternate Lady Manager.

Four eggs; two cups of sifted flour; two cups of granulated sugar; one cup of boiling water; two level teaspoonfuls of baking powder. Beat the eggs very light, yolks and whites together; add the sugar, then one cup of flour, little by little; put baking powder in the other cup of flour and add in the same way; then pour in the cup of boiling water, a little at a time, stirring constantly. Flavor with vanilla. Bake in dripping pan twenty-five minutes.

North Dakota Sponge Cake.

From MRS. ALICE VINEYARD BROWN, of North Dakota, Alternate Lady Manager.

One cup of sugar, one cup of flour, four eggs. Beat yolks of eggs to a light creamy mixture, pour over the sugar and beat two minutes; add whites beaten to a foam, and stir hard for two minutes; now add one cup of flour which has been sifted three times, and to which was added a pinch of salt; stir *very lightly*, usually four whisks of the spoon is sufficient; now pour into a shallow pan; let stand one minute; raise the pan several inches from the table and let it drop suddenly, striking flat on the bottom; this will cause air bubbles to break and make the cake fine grained; put into a very moderate oven and in five minutes heat quickly; twelve to fifteen minutes will suffice. Have ready a lemon frosting, and the result will be a most beautiful cake, fit to grace any occasion.

Alice Vineyard Brown.

Chaperone Sponge Cake.

From Mrs. Annie L. Y. Orff, of Missouri, Alternate Lady Manager.

Mix one and one-half cups pulverized sugar; one teacup flour; a little salt; one teaspoon baking powder; beat the whites of eleven eggs to a stiff froth; flavor with lemon or vanilla; mix all together and bake. Use yolks for custard or gold cake.

Annie L. Y. Orff

New England Raised Loaf Cake.

From Miss Frances S. Ives, of Connecticut, Lady Manager.

One pound of sugar, two pounds of flour, three eggs, one-fourth pound citron, one pound of butter, one pint of milk, one pound of raisins, one good-sized wine glass rum or brandy, one-half nutmeg, one cup yeast, cream one-half butter and sugar; mix this with *all* the flour, yeast and milk; let this mixture stand in a *warm* place until quite light, then add the remaining half of butter and sugar creamed and the eggs beaten very light; then let the mixture stand in a warm place until again very light; then add rum, raisins, citron and nutmeg; then put into pans for baking, letting it remain out of oven until very light again. This makes three loaves. Bake about one hour.

French Loaf Cake.

From Mrs. Martha A. Griggs, of Washington, Alternate Lady Manager.

Two and one-half cups sugar, one cup butter, one cup milk, four cups flour, three eggs, one wine glass sherry; one wine glass brandy, one-half teaspoon soda, one pound raisins (stoned), one-half pound citron, one teaspoon cloves, two teaspoons cinnamon, one nutmeg; bake one hour.

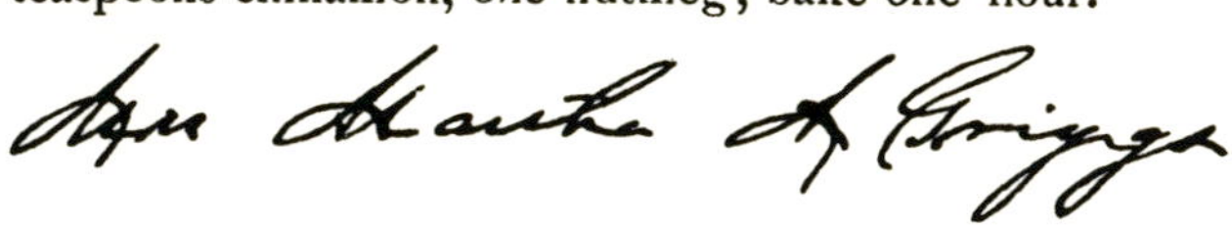

Grandmother's Bread Cake.

From Mrs. Mary C. Bell, of Florida, Lady Manager.

Three cups sugar, one cup butter, three eggs, one bowlful stoned raisins, floured, one teaspoonful allspice, ground, one teaspoonful cloves, ground, one tablespoonful cinnamon, ground. When well mixed add three cups of bread sponge before the flour is added for kneading; stir well and then add flour until as stiff as can be easily stirred; half fill two medium-sized pans and stand in a warm place till light and bake in a moderate oven.

Mary C. Bell.

Old Virginia Bread Cake.

From Mrs. Katherine S. G. Paul, of Virginia, Lady Manager.

One and one-half pounds flour; one pound white sugar; ten ounces of butter; one-half teacup sweet milk; one-half teacup good yeast; four eggs; one cup of currants and seedless raisins, chopped and mixed together; one teaspoonful each mace and cinnamon and a little allspice; work butter and sugar together; sift flour into a bowl; stir in milk and yeast with one-half the creamed butter and sugar; beat hard and long until very light; set to rise in a moderately warm place over night. In the morning, if it be well risen, work in the remainder of the butter and sugar and the eggs; dredge the fruit with flour and beat in a little at a time with the spice;

beat for fully five minutes; divide and put into two pans to rise. The second rising generally requires about three hours. When the dough is very light bake in a moderate oven. When carefully made this cake is very fine.

Bread Cake.

From Mrs. Clara L. McAdow, of Montana, Lady Manager.

Three cups of very light dough, three cups sugar, one cup butter, three eggs, one nutmeg, one teaspoonful cinnamon, raisins, a teaspoon of salaratus dissolved in a little hot water.

Corn Starch Cake.

One cup butter, two cups sugar, one teaspoon cream tartar, one-half teaspoon soda, two cups flour, one cup corn starch, four eggs, one cup milk.

Exposition Orange Cake.

From Mrs. S. E. Verdenal, of New York, Lady Manager-at-Large.

Two cups sugar, two cups of sifted flour, one-half cup of water, two teaspoonfuls yeast powder mixed with the flour, the yolks of five eggs and the whites of three beaten separately, the grating and juice of one orange; bake in layers like jelly cake.

Filling — One cup sugar, grating and juice one orange, whites of two eggs beaten into a froth.

Orange Cake.

From Mrs. Frances Welles Shepard, of Chicago, Lady Manager.

I send you with pleasure the enclosed recipe for Orange Cake. I have used it for twenty-five years and know it to be excellent. Wishing you all success in your kind efforts.

Believe me,

Yours very truly,

One coffeecup sugar, one-half coffeecup butter, two coffeecups flour, one-half coffeecup milk, yolks of four eggs, whites of two eggs, two teaspoons of baking powder; bake in four layer tins. For the filling, grate the yellow part of the rind of two oranges and mix it with the juice and one coffeecup of powdered sugar; spread this mixture between the cakes; frost the cake, using the two remaining whites of eggs beaten thoroughly, adding two small cups of powdered sugar.

Angel Food.

From MRS. MARY C. HARRISON, of Wyoming, Lady Manager.

The whites of fifteen eggs; one and one-half cups of powdered sugar; one cup of flour; one teaspoon of cream of tartar; sift sugar three times; mix cream of tartar with flour, sift seven times; beat eggs stiff, add sugar gradually, beating all the time with egg beater; take out; stir the flour quickly with wooden spoon; do not grease or line the tin; bake slowly and steadily; turn out on platter for frosting.

Mary C Harrison

Angel Cake.

From MRS. DANIEL HALL, of New Hampshire, Lady Manager.

The whites of eleven eggs beaten to a stiff froth; add one and one-half cups of pulverized sugar and one teaspoonful of vanilla extract; take one even cup of flour and one teaspoonful cream of tartar and sift with flour four times; beat lightly but thoroughly; bake fifty minutes in an ungreased pan; cut out when cold.

Sunshine Cake.

Yolks of eleven eggs, two cups of sugar, one cup of butter, one cup of milk, one teaspoonful cream tartar, one-half teaspoonful of soda, three cups of sifted flour, one teaspoonful of vanilla.

Mrs Daniel Hall.

Election Cake.

(ONE HUNDRED YEARS OLD.)

From MRS. HELEN C. BRAYTON, of South Carolina, Vice-President State Board and Lady Manager.

Four pounds flour; two pounds butter; two and one-half pounds sugar; two and one-half pounds raisins; one-half pound citron; one-half ounce mace; tumbler of brandy; one pint yeast; one and one-half pint milk; eight eggs. Add to the yeast one pint of milk; then beat in smoothly three pints of flour. Take all the flour and half the sugar and butter (when beaten to a cream); add the milk and yeast and make a dough a little softer than bread. When raised very light, add remainder of ingredients and let it rise again. When very light put into pans. Bake in moderate oven one hour.

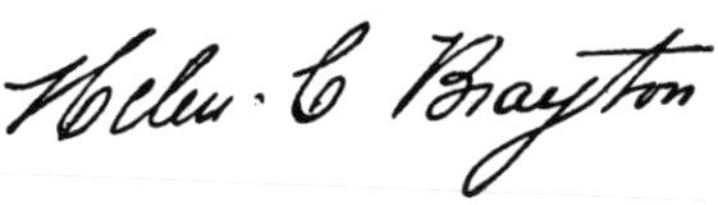

Connecticut Election Cake.

From MRS. VIRGINIA T. SMITH, of Connecticut, Alternate Lady Manager.

Two pounds best pastry flour; one pound shortening (half butter and half lard); one pound and two ounces sugar; whites of two eggs; one nutmeg; half a pound of raisins (loose Muscatels); quarter teaspoon of mace; one tablespoon of lemon juice; one tablespoon extract of orange; half teaspoon salt; half a compressed yeast cake, and two ounces of citron. Work the shortening and sugar to a cream; then rub half of it into the flour; dissolve the yeast cake in a little warm water; mix the flour and yeast with sufficient milk (about one and a half pints that has been scalded and cooled) to make a batter about like graham bread; work with the hands for at least twenty minutes; make at night and set in a moderately warm room to rise; in the morning add the remainder of the shortening and sugar; work again with the hands, as when first made, for fifteen or twenty minutes, and set to rise again. Seed and cut the raisins, grate the nutmeg and sprinkle that and the mace over the raisins. When the cake is light, add first the lemon juice, then extract of orange and whites of eggs, well beaten; stir in fruit well floured: dip into three pans, buttered and lined with paper. Let it stand until it begins to rise — it will come up very quickly in the oven if it has been twice well raised. Have oven hot enough to check the rising after it has reached the top of the pans; after it begins to brown, check the fire and let it bake rather slowly the remainder of the time. Whole time, one hour and a quarter.

Virginia T. Smith.

Almond Cream Cake.

From Mrs. Flora Beall Ginty, of Wisconsin, Seventh Vice-President Board of Lady Managers.

Two cupfuls of pulverized sugar; one-quarter cupful of butter; one cupful of sweet milk; three cupfuls of flour; two and a half teaspoonfuls of baking powder; whites of four eggs, beaten very light; one-half teaspoonful of vanilla. Bake in four layers. Whip one cupful of sweet cream to a froth, stirring gradually into it half a cupful of pulverized sugar, a few drops of vanilla, one pound of almonds, blanched and chopped fine. Spread thick between layers; frost top and sides.

Flora Beall Ginty

Velvet Cake.

From Mrs. Sallie S. Cotten, of North Carolina, President State Board and Alternate Lady Manager.

One pound sugar; one pound flour; one-half pound butter; four eggs; one teacup of cold water; one teaspoonful cream of tartar; one-half teaspoonful soda. Put yolks and whites of eggs in separate vessels; dissolve soda in the water, sift the cream tartar in the flour. Beat the sugar and butter to a white cream; add the flour and water, stirring well. Next add the whites and lastly the yolks, both well beaten. Flavor with lemon and beat all together for three minutes. Bake an hour. Excellent also for a layer cake, with any filling.

Mrs. Sallie S. Cotten.

Caramel Cake.

From Mrs. James R. Doolittle, Jr., of Chicago, Lady Manager.

One even cup butter; two even cups sugar; three even cups flour; whites of eight eggs; two even teaspoonfuls baking powder; one teaspoonful vanilla; one cup milk. Stir butter and sugar to a cream, add milk slowly, then flour in which the baking powder has been mixed, and lastly the well beaten whites of eggs and vanilla. Bake in three layers and to prevent sticking use white paper cut the size of the tin and well greased with lard.

Caramel Filling—Two cups of brown sugar; one cup of cream or milk; three tablespoonfuls butter; one teaspoonful vanilla. Boil until the mixture will hold together in water; then spread between the layers and on the outside. If it curdles when boiling, strain through coarse sieve and put on the stove again. When done, put in vanilla.

Mrs. James R. Doolittle Jr

A Caramel Cake.

From Mrs. Franc Luse Albright, of New Mexico, Lady Manager.

To be baked in layers. Four eggs; three-fourths of a cup of butter; one-half cup of milk; three and one-half cups of flour; two teaspoonfuls of baking powder; flavor to suit taste.

Filling—Two cups of brown sugar; one cup of rich cream; size of a walnut of butter; boil one-half hour well stirred; spread between the layers of the cake while hot.

Chocolate Filling—Six tablespoonfuls of grated chocolate; one and one-half cups of pulverized sugar; two tablespoonfuls of cream; put the chocolate in the pan with the cream and one-half the sugar and let dissolve; add the remainder of the sugar to the whites of two eggs well beaten; flavor with vanilla for four layers of cake.

Mrs Franc Luse Albright

Roll Jelly Cake.

From Mrs. Flora Beall Ginty, of Wisconsin, Seventh Vice-President Board of Lady Managers.

Five eggs, two cupfuls of sugar, two of flour, one-half cupful of milk, two teaspoonfuls of cream of tartar, one of soda; bake in square tins, spread with jelly and roll while warm. Lemon jelly is very nice. This recipe makes four rolls.

Flora Beall Ginty

Chocolate Cake.

From Mrs. Ralph Trautmann, of New York City, First Vice-resident Board of Lady Managers.

Have ready one-half pound sweet chocolate grated; one-fourth pound chopped citron; one-fourth pound almonds, blanched and chopped; five soda crackers, browned and rolled very fine; wineglass of brandy and the juice and grated rind of two lemons; separate the yolks of eggs from the whites; beat yolks well, mix with other ingredients and lastly add the whites whipped to a stiff froth; bake two hours in a slow oven; cover with frosting and ornament with candied fruit.

Mary. E. Trautmann

Georgie's Cake.

From Mrs. Clark Waring, of South Carolina, Alternate Lady Manager.

Three teaspoonfuls of soda; one cup butter; one cup molasses; two cups brown sugar; two cups sour milk; four eggs; four and one-half cups flour; one tablespoonful mixed spices; two pounds dates, seeded and chopped fine; rub the butter and sugar to a cream, add the molasses, then the sour milk, break one egg in at a time and beat well; sift the soda in the flour and add, saving a little to dust the dates; add the spices and last of all add the dates; bake slowly like a fruit cake.

Mrs Clark Waring

Chess Cake.

From MRS. CARRINGTON MASON, of Tennessee, Alternate Lady Manager.

Four eggs beaten separately and added to one cup of butter and one cup of sugar thoroughly creamed, flavor with nutmeg; line small patty pans with puff paste; place in the bottom a teaspoonful of jelly and pour over it a tablespoonful of the egg, butter and sugar mixture; bake in a rather slow oven. This is a nice tart for lunch or picnics as it keeps well and never gets dry.

Mrs. Carrington Mason.

Fruit Cake.

From MRS. A. K. DELANEY, of Alaska, Lady Manager.

One and one-half pound of flour; one and one-half pound of sugar; one and one-fourth pound of butter; two pounds of raisins; two pounds of currants; three-fourths pound candied lemon, four nutmegs; one teaspoonful soda; one teaspoonful cinnamon; one teaspoonful cloves; one cup brandy or wine; bake slowly.

Mrs A. K. Delany

English Fruit Cake.

From Mrs. Phœbe M. Hartpence, of Ohio, Chairman Commissioners on Woman's Work, Lady Manager.

Four cups brown sugar; two cups butter; twelve eggs; one lemon, grated; two nutmegs, grated; one-half tablespoonful cloves; one tablespoonful cinnamon; one tablespoonful allspice; one-half pint cream; one cup pure brandy; eight cups flour, sifted; one-half cup molasses; two and one-half pounds raisins, seeded, whole; two and one-half pounds currants; six teaspoonfuls baking powder; one level teaspoonful soda. The success of this cake depends very largely upon having every ingredient prepared before commencing to use them. Begin by thoroughly mixing sugar and butter, then yolks of eggs well beaten; put the soda into the molasses and cream, add this to the above; next add spices and stir up thoroughly; now add the brandy (good whisky will do); take a portion of the flour and thoroughly flour the fruit with it; put the baking powder in the flour that remains and sift part of it into the mixture; now add the beaten whites of eggs and stir gently; stir in the fruit, bake from two to two and one-half hours in a moderate oven.

Phoebe M. Hartpence.

Fruit Cake.

From Mrs. M. P. H. Beeson, of Oklahoma, Lady Manager.

Yolks of one dozen eggs, one pound dried currants, one pound seeded raisins, one pound butter, one - half pound citron, one pound brown sugar, one cup sorghum molasses, one pound blanched almonds, one - half pound Brazil nuts, one - half cup sour milk, two teaspoonfuls soda, six cups flour, with cinnamon, allspice and cloves. The flour should be browned in slow oven in order to make the cake look dark and rich. This recipe will make a very large cake, the same to be baked for three hours in slow oven.

Fruit Cake.

From Mrs Hester A. Hanback, of Kansas, Lady Manager.

One pound butter, one pound brown sugar, one pound flour, twelve eggs, four pounds currants, four pounds raisins, one pound citron, two pounds figs, two pounds blanched almonds, two oranges, one tablespoonful cinnamon, one tablespoonful allspice, one - half tablespoonful mace, one - half tablespoonful cloves, one nutmeg, one lemon peel (chopped fine), one gill wine, one gill brandy; chop orange peel and pulp (removing seeds), then work in all the sugar you can (this is extra sugar), slice the almonds thin, also citron, chop figs quite fine. Fruit should be weighed after seeding and currants washed. Beat whites and yolks of eggs separately and roll fruit in flour before putting together. This makes a ten quart pan full. One tablespoonful baking powder; five pounds raisins, four pounds seeded; four and one - fourth pounds currants, four pounds washed; six pounds almonds, two pounds blanched.

Sally White Cake.

From MRS. FLORENCE H. KIDDER, of North Carolina, Lady Manager.

The "Sally White Cake" is delicious, and if I am not mistaken, has yet only a local fame, but it should have a national one. Wishing you every success in your undertaking, I am,

Very sincerely yours,

One pound of butter, three pounds of citron, one and one-fourth pound of sugar, one pound of flour, fifteen eggs, two small cocoanuts grated, one and one-half pound of almonds, blanched and pounded (weigh after blanching), one nutmeg, one tablespoonful of mace, one wineglass of best brandy, one of Madeira or sherry, bake slowly as a fruit cake and frost.

Delicate Cake.

From MRS. JOHN A. LOGAN, of District of Columbia, Lady Manager.

Four ounces butter, fourteen ounces sugar, whites of six eggs, twelve ounces of flour, two teaspoons of baking powder, one cup of milk. Rub the butter and sugar together until they form a cream, stir the baking powder through the

MRS. JOHN A. LOGAN.

flour, then add it, a cupful at a time, to the butter and sugar, then stir in the milk, putting in the whites of the eggs after being beaten to a froth, a large spoonful at a time. Bake in a brisk oven.

Mrs. John A. Logan

Delicate Cake.

From Mrs. Harriet T. Upton, of Ohio, Alternate Lady Manager.

Use the same size cup for all ingredients. Two cups (coffee) sugar, one-half cup butter, stir to a cream; whites of eight eggs beaten stiff, three-fourths cup sweet milk, two and one-half cups flour, two teaspoons baking powder stirred into flour; put whites of eggs in last and stir gently.

Harriet T. Upton

White Cake.

From Mrs. Governor John M. Stone, of Mississippi, Lady Manager.

Whites of twelve eggs, five teacups flour, three teacups sugar, one teacup sweet milk, one full cup butter, two teaspoonfuls yeast powder.

Mrs. John M. Stone.

Walnut Cake.

From Mrs. Frances C. Holley, of North Dakota, Alternate Lady Manager.

Three cups of sugar; one cup of butter; four cups of flour; one and one-half cup of sweet milk; three cups of walnut or butternut meats; whites of eight eggs. Cream the butter and sugar; sift two teaspoons of cream tartar into the flour, into which stir the meats. Dissolve one teaspoon of soda in the milk. Salt and extract as you like, adding the thoroughly-whipped whites the last thing before putting into the oven. Half of this rule can be used.

Frances C. Holley

Nut Cake.

From Miss Josephine Shakspeare, of Louisiana, Lady Manager.

Four tablespoons of flour; four tablespoons of *brown* sugar; one tablespoon of butter; one egg; one teacup of chopped nuts; a pinch of salt and black pepper. Grease and heat a long biscuit pan, mix all ingredients well and spread thinly on heated pan. Bakes in a few moments. When done and while warm, run a knife through center of pan lengthwise, then crosswise in strips. Turn pan over, and when cool cakes should be quite crisp. Very old French recipe.

Josephine Shakspeare.

Nut Cake.

From MRS. MINNA G. HOOKER, of Vermont, Alternate Lady Manager.

One-half cup butter; two cups sugar; one cup milk; three cups flour; four eggs; one pint nut meats; two teaspoons baking powder. Cream butter and sugar. Add eggs well whipped, milk, flour with baking powder, and nut meats chopped fine. Bake in loaf. English walnuts best.

Nut Cake.

From MRS. ALICE HOUGHTON, of Washington, Lady Manager.

One and one-half cup sugar; one-half cup butter; whites of six eggs, beaten stiff; one-half cup milk; one and two-thirds cup flour; one-third cup corn starch; one teaspoon baking powder; one and one-half pound English walnuts, chopped fine and floured. Bake slowly in moderate oven.

Pecan Cake.

From MRS. RUSSELL B. HARRISON, of Montana, Vice-President-at-Large.

One cup of butter; two and a half cups of flour; two cups of sugar; one-half cup of sweet milk; whites of eight eggs; two teaspoonfuls baking powder. Beat together butter and sugar; add a little of the beaten egg; then put in a cup of flour, then some milk, then again flour and milk; put all the milk in with the second cup of flour; then add the rest of the egg.

Icing to fill and put over top of Pecan Cake—Whites of six eggs, beaten stiff with powdered sugar; one small can of grated pineapple and two cups of pecans, chopped fine. The nuts should soak awhile in the pineapple before mixing them into the egg and sugar. Put whole pecan kernels over the top of the cake while the icing is still soft.

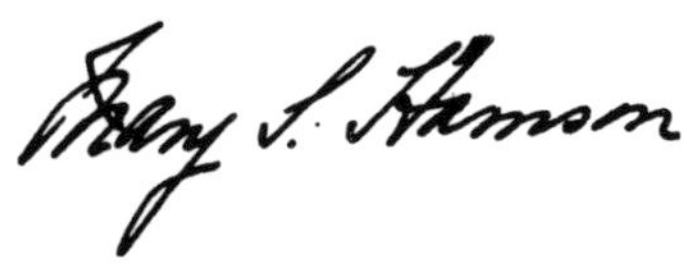

Cake Made with Cream.

From MRS. SARAH H. BIXBY, of Maine, Alternate Lady Manager.

Break two eggs in a cup and fill with cream, and one cup sugar, one teaspoonful cream tartar, one-half teaspoonful soda and one and one-half cup of flour, with a little salt.

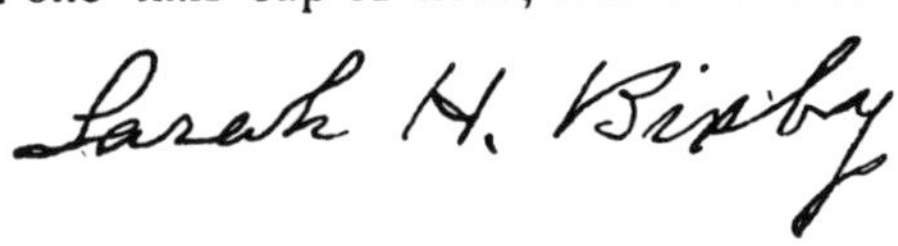

Cream Frosting.

From MRS. MARY PAYTON, of Oregon, Lady Manager.

One cup of sweet thick cream, sweetened and flavored with vanilla. Cut a loaf of cake in two and spread the

MRS. RUSSELL B. HARRISON.

frosting between and on top. This tastes like Charlotte Russe.

Mary Payton.

Almond Icing.

From Mrs. Lana A. Bates, of Nebraska, Alternate Lady Manager.

Whites of four eggs; one pound of sweet almonds; one pound powdered sugar; a little rose water. Blanch the almonds by pouring boiling water over them and stripping off the skins. When dry, pound them to a paste, a few at a time, in a mortar, moistening with rose water as you go on. When beaten fine and smooth, beat gradually into icing. Put on the cake very thick and when nearly dry cover with plain icing.

Lana A. Bates

Soft Gingerbread.

From Mrs. Ida M. Ball, of Delaware, Lady Manager.

One teacup sweet milk, one teacup brown sugar, one teacup butter or mixed butter and lard, one teacup molasses, one tablespoonful ginger, one tablespoonful cinnamon, four cups flour, two eggs, one pound of raisins, well floured before being put in, two teaspoonfuls baking powder.

Ida M. Ball.

Columbian Ginger Cake.

From Mrs. S. E. Verdenal, of New York, Lady Manager-at-Large.

One cup molasses, one cup sugar, one-half cup water, one-half cup lard, one teaspoonful soda, season with ginger or cinnamon, put flour in until stiff enough to roll out thin and cut into small cakes.

Gingerbread.

From Mrs. Sam. S. Fifield, of Wisconsin, Alternate Lady Manager.

One-half cup of molasses, one-half cup of sugar, one-half cup of butter, one-half cup of sour milk, one and one-half cup of flour, two small eggs, one-half teaspoon of soda, teaspoonful of cinnamon, ginger, and one-half teaspoon of cloves, a little nutmeg.

Soft Gingerbread.

From Mrs. Mary R. Kinder, of Delaware, Lady Manager.

One cupful of molasses, one of butter, one of sugar, one of sour cream, one tablespoonful of ginger, three eggs, one dessertspoonful of soda, ground spice according to taste, and one quart of sifted flour. Mix the butter and sugar to a cream, then add the other ingredients.

Mary H. Kinder.

Loaf Ginger Cake.

From Mrs. A. K. Delaney, of Alaska, Lady Manager.

Two eggs, one-half cup molasses, two-thirds cup sugar, half cup lard or butter, one-half cup milk, three cups flour, one tablespoon ginger, one teaspoonful cinnamon, one-half tablespoonful soda dissolved in boiling water, stir in quickly and put in the oven at once.

Mrs A. K. Delany

COOKIES

Hermits or Fruit Cookies.

From MRS. SUSAN G. COOKE, of Tennessee, Secretary of the Board of Lady Managers.

I take pleasure in sending you the enclosed recipes. I thought if anyone should send you a recipe for Cookies it ought to be myself. I anticipate spending many pleasant hours in the hereafter trying the recipes of our well known Lady Managers. With best wishes, believe me always, Most cordially yours.

Susan G. Cooke

Three eggs, one and one-half cup sugar, one cup butter, one large cup of raisins stoned and chopped, one teaspoon soda; one teaspoon cloves, one teaspoon allspice, one teaspoon cinnamon, flour enough to roll.

Cookies.

From MISS LILY IRENE JACKSON, of West Virginia, Lady Manager.

Three eggs, two cups of sugar, one cup of butter, one cup of sweet milk, two teaspoons baking powder mix soft, roll thin, bake in a quick oven.

Lily Irene Jackson.

MRS. SUSAN G COOKE

"Corinita" Cookies.

From Miss Lucia B. Perea, of New Mexico, Alternate Lady Manager.

One cup sugar, one-fourth cup butter, three eggs well beaten together, one cup milk, two teaspoonfuls baking powder well sifted in two cups flour.

Cookies.

From Mrs. Robt. B. Mitchell, of Kansas, Lady Manager.

Beat to a cream one cup of butter, two and one-half cups of sugar and the yolks of two eggs. Add a cup of sour cream, into which has been dissolved a small teaspoonful of soda; beat the whites of four eggs to a stiff froth; add to the butter and sugar; flavor to taste; use as little flour as possible to make of consistency to roll thin; sprinkle with sugar; flour the cutter to keep dough from sticking; bake in quick oven.

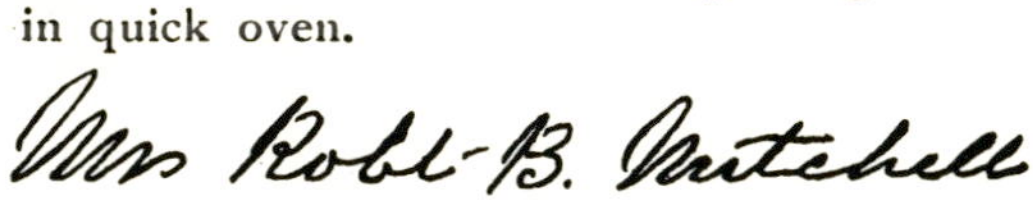

Ginger Cookies.

From Mrs. Clara L. McAdow, of Montana, Lady Manager.

Two tumblers molasses, one tumbler sweet milk, one tumbler butter, one tablespoon soda, one tablespoon ginger. Well beaten. Mix very soft. Roll *thick*. Bake in a quick oven.

Ginger Snaps.

From Mrs. Sam. S. Fifield, of Wisconsin, Alternate Lady Manager.

One cup of lard, one cup of molasses, one cup of sugar, one teaspoonful of ginger, one teaspoonful of soda, dissolved in a little water. Boil the sugar, molasses and lard three minutes, let cool, then add the other ingredients and flour to make very stiff. Bake in a hot oven.

Mrs Sam S. Fifield

French Jumbles.

From Mrs. E. S. Thomson, of Maryland, Lady Manager.

One and one-half pounds of flour, one pound of granulated sugar, three-quarters of a pound of butter, three eggs, one teaspoonful of baking soda, dissolved in half a cup of milk. Season with lemon and grated nutmeg to taste. Roll with your hand in granulated sugar. Make in small rings and bake on tin sheets in a quick oven. The dough should be soft as it can be handled.

E. S. Thomson

Sand Tarts.

From Miss Eloise L. Roman, of Maryland, Alternate Lady Manager.

To three-quarters of a pound of butter, well creamed, add one pound of sugar and three eggs, reserving the white of one; stir in one pound of flour. Roll out thin and spread on the white of egg; sprinkle with cinnamon and sugar, and cut in squares. Have a half-pound of blanched and quartered almonds and place on the squares. Bake quickly.

Eloise L. Roman

Lady Fingers.

From Mrs. M. D. Owings, of Washington, Lady Manager.

Mix into a half pound of confectioner's sugar the yolks of six eggs. Work this mixture with a spoon until very light and frothy; then mix into it the whites of six eggs that have been beaten stiff, adding at the same time a quarter of a pound of flour, dried and sifted. Place this batter into a meringue bag, and squeeze it through in strips two and one-half inches long, sprinkle over some fine sugar and bake in a moderate oven twelve to fifteen minutes.

M. D. Owings

DESSERTS

CREAMS JELLIES CUSTARDS

Pineapple Sponge.

From Mrs. Matilda B. Carse, of Chicago, Lady Manager.

Soak one-half package gelatine in one-half cup water for two hours; to a pint and a half can of pineapple add one cup of sugar and one cup of water; simmer fifteen minutes; add the gelatine and allow to remain over the fire until the gelatine is all melted; pour into a *tin* basin and place in ice water; when thoroughly cold and beginning to thicken add the juice of one lemon and the stiffly beaten whites of four eggs; beat until it will just pour, then turn into a mould and set in a cool place to harden. Serve next day with whipped cream, sweetened with powdered sugar and flavored with a few drops of vanilla.

Matilda B. Carse

Pineapple Soufflé.

From Mrs. James R. Deane, of California, Lady Manager.

Three ounces pineapple, cut in discs; three ounces sifted flour; three ounces sugar; two ounces butter; one-half pint of milk; yolks of three eggs; whites of four eggs. Melt butter in a stew pan, add the flour and milk and cook well; add the sugar and pineapple; add the yolks of eggs, one by one, and stir well; then add the whites of eggs whipped to a stiff froth; stir these in lightly; pour into a well-greased soufflée tin; steam one hour over water that just simmers, not boiling. Serve with this sauce: Reduce one glass pine-apple syrup about one-half; add one ounce cube sugar and one glass sherry; color with cochineal and oour around the pudding.

Mrs. James R. Deane

Peach Sponge.

From Mrs. Joseph C. Straughan, of Idaho, Lady Manager.

One pint of canned peaches, one-half package of gelatine, the whites of five eggs, one scant cupful of sugar, one and a half cupful of water; soak the gelatine for two hours in half a cupful of the water; boil the cupful of the water and sugar fifteen minutes; mash the peaches fine, rub through a sieve and put in the syrup, cook five minutes, stirring all the time; place the sauce pan in another of boiling water and add the gelatine; stir for five or eight minutes to dissolve the gelatine; then place the sauce pan in a dish of ice water and beat the syrup until it begins to cool; add the whites of the eggs and beat until the mixture begins to harden; pour into a mould and set away to harden; serve with cream and sugar.

Mrs. Joseph C. Straughan

Hamburg Cream.

From Mrs. Ida M. Ball, of Delaware, Lady Manager.

Beat together the juice of two lemons, half pound of sifted sugar, yolks of five eggs; put on the fire in a double boiler and let it come to a boil; add quickly the whites of the eggs beaten stiff; stir all well together; take immediately from the fire and serve cold in glasses or in large dessert dish.

Chocolat Moussé.

From Miss Josephine Shakspeare, of Louisiana, Lady Manager

Four strips of chocolate, one quart of milk, six eggs, one tablespoon of corn starch; sweeten to taste, and vanilla flavoring. Chocolate dissolved in a little warm milk to a paste. Put milk on to boil and stir in chocolate gradually. Set saucepan where it will cook slowly. Beat eggs well, mix in corn starch and add to milk and chocolate. Boil gently until smooth and thick, stirring until done. Pour into glass dish, or custard cups. To be eaten cold with sweetened whipped cream, heaped upon it.

Chocolat Soufflé.

From Mrs. Alice Houghton, of Washington, Lady Manager.

One pint milk, two tablespoons corn starch, one cup sugar, one square grated chocolate, three eggs (yolks).

MRS. J. FRANK BALL.

Scald the milk and stir in the corn starch wet in a little cold milk, add sugar to the chocolate and dissolve in a little boiling water, stir into the milk and when cooked add the beaten yolks of three eggs. Remove from the fire and flavor with vanilla. When cold pour over the top one cup whipped cream, to which has been added the beaten whites of three eggs.

Alice Houghton.

Chocolat Meringue.

From Mrs. Katharine S. G. Paul, of Virginia, Lady Manager.

One teacupful grated chocolate, one pint warm water. Boil together. Then add one pint sweet milk and let come to a boil. Add two heaping tablespoonfuls of corn starch, dissolved in one-half cup of milk, sweeten to taste and when cool flavor with vanilla. Beat the whites of two eggs and a pinch of pulverized sugar to a very light froth, and pile on top.

Katharine S. G. Paul

Bavarian Cream.

From Mrs. Alice J. Whalen, of Utah Territory, Lady Manager.

One-half box gelatine, one-half cup cold water, one pint cream, one pint milk, four eggs (yolks), one-half cup sugar, one-half teaspoonful salt, one teaspoonful vanilla, one tablespoonful wine. Soak the gelatine in cold water till soft. Chill and whip the cream till you have three pints. Keep the whipped cream on ice, and boil the remainder of the cream, adding enough milk to make a pint in all. Beat the yolks of the eggs, and add the sugar and salt. Pour the boiling milk on the eggs, and when well mixed put back in the double boiler and cook about two minutes, or just enough to scald the egg. Stir constantly, add the soaked gelatine, and strain at once into a pan set in ice water. When cool, add the vanilla and wine. Stir until it begins to harden, then stir in quickly the whipped cream, and when nearly stiff enough to drop, pour into moulds wet in cold water.

Chocolate Bavarian Cream—Melt two sticks of sweetened chocolate, and stir them into the custard before straining.

Alice J. Whalen

Gelatine Cream.

From Miss Mary Elliott McCandless, of Pennsylvania, Lady Manager.

To a pint of cream add half a cupful of powdered sugar and a teaspoonful vanilla extract; whip it to a stiff froth; dissolve a quarter of a box of gelatine in two wine glasses of sherry heated, but not allowed to boil; let this cool a little, then stir into the cream; pour the whole in a mould and set it on the ice to stiffen.

Mary Elliott McCandless

Nob Hill Pudding.

From Miss Lida M. Russell, of Nevada, Lady Manager.

For one pint thick cream dissolve four sheets of isinglass in four tablespoons of hot water; whip cream until thick, sweeten and flavor; have isinglass warm enough to pour, but not too hot; stir in very fast and put in mould to cool.

Apple Charlotte.

From Mrs. John A. Logan, District of Columbia, Lady Manager.

Mix one pint of stewed apples with one cup of sugar; the grated rind and juice of one lemon; soak one-third of a box of gelatine in one-third of a cup of cold water twenty minutes; add one-third of a cup of boiling water to dissolve the gelatine; when cool add it to the apples; when beginning to stiffen add the beaten whites of three eggs; pour into moulds lined with lady fingers; serve with soft custard poured round the base of the charlotte.

Charlotte de Russe.

From Mrs. Charles Price, of North Carolina, Third Vice-President Board Lady Managers.

One pint rich cream; two eggs; one-quarter ounce of gelatine; sherry wine. Whip cream, first sweetening with a cup of pulverized sugar, adding enough sherry to flavor and the yolk of one egg. Whip stiff the two whites of the eggs. Dissolve gelatine in half a cup of milk. Line glass dish with slices of sponge cake or lady fingers. Whip all the ingredients together and pour in dish to congeal.

Mrs Charles Force.

Charlotte Russe.

From Mrs. Marcia Louise Gould, of Illinois, President State Board and Lady Manager.

Whip one quart of rich cream to a stiff froth and drain well on a sieve. To one scant pint of milk add eggs beaten very light. Make very sweet and flavor with vanilla. Cook over hot water till it is a thick custard. Soak one full ounce of Cox's gelatine in a *little* cold water; warm over hot water. When the custard is *very* cold, beat in lightly the gelatine and the whipped cream. Line the bottom of your mould with buttered paper, the sides with sponge cake or lady fingers, fastened together with the white of an egg. Fill with the cream and put in a cold place, in the summer on the ice. To turn out, dip the mold for a moment in *hot* water.

Marcia Louise Gould

Charlotte Russe.

From Mrs. Susan W. Ball, of Indiana, Alternate Lady Manager.

One-half box gelatine, put to soak in one-half pint of milk for an hour. Take one-half pint of milk and yolks of two eggs and make a custard, sweeten and flavor to taste; when thick enough, stir in the gelatine until cool. Take one quart rich cream, flavored with wine; sweeten and whip; two dozen lady fingers, soaked in wine; line a bowl with them. When the custard is cold, stir the cream in it, continuing to stir until it begins to harden; then pour into bowl. If the cream is not very rich, add the whites of two eggs.

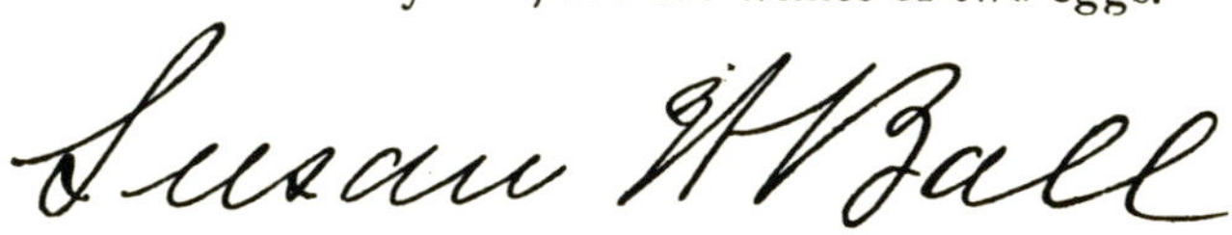

Charlotte Russe.

From Mrs. George W. Lamar, of Georgia, Alternate Lady Manager.

One quart of cream; sweeten and flavor with two wineglasses of wine and a half teaspoonful of vanilla. Whip with an egg whip until it becomes very thick. Put one-third of a box of gelatine (Nelson's preferred) to soak in one pint of water. When quite soft pour off the water and dissolve by holding over the fire and stirring carefully; when tepid pour into the cream. Let the mixture congeal partially and pour into a mould that has been lined with lady fingers or sponge cake cut into strips. Put into a cold place and turn out before serving.

Strawberry Blanc Mange.

From Mrs. Benedette B. Tobin, of Texas, President State Board and Lady Manager.

Crush slightly with a silver spoon a quart (measured without their stalks) of fresh and finely flavored strawberries; strew over them eight ounces of powdered sugar and let them stand three or four hours, then turn them onto a fine hair sieve reversed, and rub them through it. Melt over a gentle fire two ounces of best gelatine in a pint of new milk and sweeten it with four ounces of sugar; strain it through a fine muslin bag and then mix it with a pint and a quarter of sweet thick cream; keep stirring until nearly or quite cold, then pour it gradually on the strawberries, whisking briskly together. Last of all add in small portions the strained juice of a fine large lemon. Mould blanc mange and set in a very cold place for twelve hours or more before serving. Strawberries, one quart; sugar, eight ounces; gelatine, two ounces; new milk, one pint; sugar, four ounces; cream, one and one-fourth pint; juice one lemon.

Benedette B. Tobin

Snow Pudding.

From Mrs. Susan G. Cooke, of Tennessee, Secretary of the Board of Lady Managers.

One-half package gelatine, three eggs, juice of one lemon, one pint of milk, two cups sugar; soak the gelatine one hour in a teacup cold water; to this add one pint of boiling water (at the end of hour); stir until gelatine is thoroughly dissolved; add two-thirds of the sugar and lemon juice; beat the whites of eggs to a stiff froth. When the gelatine is quite cold, whip into the whites, a spoonful at a time, for at least one hour; whip steadily, and when all is stiff, pour into a mould previously wet with cold water; set in a cold place; when sufficiently moulded turn into a glass dish. Make a custard of the milk, eggs and remainder of the sugar, flavor with vanilla or bitter almond and pour this around the base of mould before serving.

Susan G. Cooke

Wine or Gelatine Jelly.

From MRS. CARRINGTON MASON, of Tennessee, Alternate Lady Manager.

To a box of Cox or Nelson's gelatine, put a pint of cold water, the juice of three lemons and the rind of one: let it stand one hour, then add three pints of boiling water, one and one half pound white sugar, one tumbler of Madeira or sherry wine; stir all the ingredients well together and strain through a jelly bag.

Mrs. Carrington Mason

Fruit Jelly.

From MISS WILHELMINE REITZ, of Indiana, Lady Manager.

Cover one box of gelatine with a half pint of cold water and stand it aside for thirty minutes, then pour over it one pint of boiling water, add one pound of sugar, juice of three lemons and two oranges, strain. Moisten a plain mould with cold water, put in the bottom a layer of white grapes, pour in a little of the gelatine; stand on ice until the gelatine congeals. Now put a layer of candied cherries, then a layer of sliced bananas, a layer of orange pulp, another layer of bananas, then a layer of chopped almonds, another layer of grapes and so continue until the mould is full. Pour over this the remaining quantity of gelatine, which must be perfectly cold but not stiff; stand away to harden. If you use wine, the gelatine may be flavored with wine omitting the orange and lemon.

Wilhelmine Reitz

A Dainty Dessert.

From MRS. SOLOMON THATCHER, JR, of Illinois, Lady Manager.

Take choice Seville oranges, remove carefully about one-third of the orange, leaving a strip one-half inch wide to form a handle. From this improvised orange basket carefully scoop all the pulp, leaving only the empty shell. Fill this full of Charlotte Russe. This makes a pretty dish.

Clara E Thatcher

Tamales de Dulce.

From SEÑORA DON MANUEL CHAVES, of New Mexico.

Para hacer tamales de dulce se descojo buen mais blanco y se hace nistamal. Despues se lava muy bien de modo que no le quede. nada cal y se muele en el metate muy remolido. Despues se bate la masa en un cajete bien batida y sepulsa en una poca de agua hasta el ver que esta bien alsado. Cuando la masa se sube sobre el agua ya esta de punto. Se le echa una poca de manteca y asucar y se les pone adatro una poca de canela molida y pasas y se enbuelven en ojas de mais, y se amarran y ya estan listos para ser cosidos con vapor.

Visenta Lavadi de Chaves

A Cheap Dessert.

From MRS. KATE CANTHON McDANIEL, of Texas, Lady Manager.

Beat the whites of four eggs to a stiff froth; place them carefully in a vessel containing a pint of boiling milk; let them remain until set, then remove carefully to a plate. Beat the four yolks and a cup of sugar until light; stir in half cup of sweet milk, pour slowly into the boiling milk, stirring briskly all the while; continue stirring and let it remain on the fire long enough to thicken, taking care that it never boils or it will be unfit for use; flavor to suit the taste. Place slices of any cake in dessert plates; pour the custard over them, put a spoonful of the whites on each piece of cake and a drop of jelly in the center of the whites.

Kate Canthon, McDaniel

Bananas in Jelly.

From MRS. GOVERNOR RICKARDS, of Montana, President State Board and Lady Manager.

Make with boiling water one quart of strong lemonade, using only the juice of the lemons; soak one-half box of gelatine in a small cup of cold water; stir it into the boiling lemonade and set where it will cool but not harden. Cut three bananas in length-wise halves and lay them in a mould wet with cold water, cover with one-half the jelly and put the mould on ice till jelly is set, then slice three more and pour on remainder of jelly. Serve with cream or soft custard.

Eliza A. Richards

Almond Blanc Mange.

From MRS. BENEDETTE B. TOBIN, of Texas, President State Board and Lady Manager.

One quart of milk, one ounce of gelatine, three ounces almonds blanched and pounded in a mortar with one tablespoon of rose water added to prevent oiling; three-fourths cup sugar. Heat the milk to boiling, having previously soaked the gelatine in a cup of it for an hour, add gelatine when the milk is scalding hot, add the pounded almond paste and stir all together ten minutes before putting in the sugar. When the gelatine has dissolved remove the blanc mange from the vessel of boiling water in which you have cooked it, and strain through a thin muslin bag, pressing it well to get flavor of almonds—there should be three or four bitter ones among them. Wet a mould with cold water, put in the blanc mange and set in a cold place until firm.

Benedette B. Tobin

Floating Island.

From Mrs. Rosine Ryan, of Texas, Lady Manager-at-Large.

Break six eggs into a bowl, separating the whites from four with the yolks and whites of two; make a boiled custard, say a quart of milk, six tablespoonfuls of sugar, a flavoring of vanilla, peach or sherry wine. Beat the whites to a stiff froth, sweetening and flavoring them a little also. Wet a large spoon, turn it around in the beaten eggs, take out a piece of oblong shape, and poach it in boiling milk. When the custard is cold, pour it into a glass dish and place the poached whites on top.

Rosine Ryan

Boiled Custard.

From Mrs. Charles J. McClung, of Tennessee, Alternate Lady Manager.

Let one quart of milk come to a boil with a piece of stick cinnamon in it. Beat six eggs (leaving out the whites of three for the float) and one half pint of sugar very light and pour the boiling milk into them. Wash your kettle and return all to the stove and boil until as thick as cream (be sure and do not boil until curdled), then set aside to cool. Beat the whites of three eggs with three tablespoonfuls of sugar, to which you add a little acid jelly as you beat; beat until perfectly smooth and put on the top of your custard in spoonfuls.

Mrs Charles J. McClung

Snow Balls.

From Mrs. Nancy Huston Banks, of Kentucky, Alternate Lady Manager-at-Large.

One cup white sugar, one cup thick cream, whites of five eggs, two teaspoonfuls baking powder, flour to make a stiff batter; bake in small custard cups.

Nancy Huston Banks

Lemon Custard.

From Mrs. Ida M. Ball, of Delaware, Lady Manager.

One lemon (juice and grated rind), one cup sugar, yolks of two eggs, one teaspoonful butter, one-half cup water, two teaspoonfuls cornstarch, boil water and stir in above mixture.

Icing for top — Whites of two eggs, two tablespoonfuls of pulverized sugar.

Ida M. Ball

ICE CREAM

Fruit Cream.

From Mrs. H. F. Brown, of Minnesota, Lady Manager.

One quart of fruit (after being put through colander); one cup of cold water — very sweet. Add the whites of three eggs (unbeaten). Put in a freezer and freeze as ice cream, stirring continually.

Mrs. H. F. Brown.

Caramel Ice Cream.

From Mrs. Lily Rosecrans Toole, of Montana, Lady Manager.

Take one pint of brown sugar and *burn* it; then add water, making a dark brown fluid. This ought to make enough to flavor three pints of cream. Have the cream very rich, more so than for ordinary ice cream. Then color the cream with the caramel until it is a good shade of brown — darker than coffee color. For this you must have your caramel very black, as it is the quality and not the quantity of caramel that will give the proper flavor; sweeten to taste.

Lily Rosecrans Toole

Tutti Frutti Ice Cream.

From Mrs. J. Montgomery Smith, of Wisconsin, Alternate Lady Manager.

Make one quart rich vanilla ice cream, and when partly frozen, add one pound of candied fruit, either cherries, currants or citron.

Mrs J. Montgomery Smith

Vanilla Ice Cream.

From Mrs. Mary C. Harrison, of Wyoming, Lady Manager.

Three quarts sweet cream; one quart powdered sugar; one pint sweet milk (dissolve sugar in milk); two tablespoons extract vanilla. Pack with equal quantities of cracked ice and rock salt. Turn slowly and steadily.

Mary C Harrison

Maraschino Ice Cream.

From Miss Mary Elliott McCandless, of Pennsylvania, Lady Manager.

A simple rule for Maraschino ice cream calls for one quart of cream, a large cup of granulated sugar, six egg yolks, a cup of milk, and a tablespoonful of gelatine, which has been soaked for two hours in four tablespoonfuls of cold water. Let the milk come to a boil and pour it slowly over the eggs, beat them all the while to prevent their curdling. Then add the gelatine and finally the sugar. Beat the whole well, strain it into the cream and add four tablespoonfuls of Maraschino. Pack the cream in a freezer and freeze like any other. When it is of proper consistency, remove the beater, cork up the freezer, pack in more ice and salt, cover the whole closely with thick newspapers and let it rest for an hour or two before it is served. This is a most delicious cream.

Mary Elliott McCandless

CANDY

Chocolate Caramels.

From Mrs. Carrington Mason, of Tennessee, Alternate Lady Manager.

One pound white sugar; one-quarter pound chocolate; four tablespoonfuls of molasses; one cup of sweet milk, and a piece of butter the size of a walnut. Boil until it will harden in water. Flavor with vanilla and pour on a buttered slab.

Mrs. Carrington Mason

Fudges.

From Mrs. J. Montgomery Smith, of Wisconsin, Alternate Lady Manager.

Four cups granulated sugar; one cup cream; one cup water; one-half cake chocolate; one-half cup butter. Cook until it just holds together, then add two teaspoonfuls extract of vanilla and pour into pans, not buttered. When cool enough to bear finger in, stir it until it no longer runs. It should not grain, but be smooth. Cut into squares.

Mrs J. Montgomery Smith

Cream Candy.

From Mrs. Mary Payton, of Oregon, Lady Manager.

Stir into the white of one egg and one tablespoonful of water, sugar (confectioner's) enough to make into molds. Press one-half walnut on each side and place in a dry place. Dates can be used in the same way as the nuts.

Mary Payton.

PUNCH

Romaine.

From Mrs. Potter Palmer, of Chicago, President Board of Lady Managers

With best wishes for your success, I am
Very sincerely yours,

Bertha Honoré Palmer

Boil together one quart of water and one pint of sugar for about half an hour; add the juice of six good sized lemons and one orange; strain and set away to cool. Then prepare the following: Boil together one gill of sugar and one gill of water for eighteen minutes. While the syrup is cooking, beat the whites of four eggs very stiff, and into these pour the hot syrup very slowly—beating all the time, and continue to beat a few minutes after it is all in. Set this away to cool. Place the first mixture in the freezer and freeze by turning it all the time for twenty minutes. Then take off the cover, remove the beater and add one gill of sherry, two tablespoonfuls Jamaica rum and the meringue, mixing this well with a spoon into the frozen preparation. Cover again and set away until time to serve.

Serve in punch glasses, as a course between entrées and roast.

Roman Punch.

From MRS. JOHN R. WILSON, of South Dakota, Lady Manager.

Three pounds pulverized sugar; three quarts of water; the juice of eight lemons. Soak two tablespoonfuls of gelatine in a little of the water; boil all together for a moment, then cool and strain; add one-half pint of rum and the whites of eight eggs *without beating*. Freeze.

Kirsch Punch.

Place in a vessel half a pound of powderd sugar, with one quart of cold water; grate in the rind of a large lemon or of two smaller ones, squeezing in the juice of three good-sized ones, or four, if small. Beat this thoroughly for five minutes. Taste the mixture and add more powdered sugar if desired sweeter; then strain through a sieve into the freezer. Stir into this two gills of Kirsch. Freeze it as you would an ice cream. Serve in twelve punch glasses.

Abricot Sorbet.

From MRS. M. D. OWINGS, of Washington, Lady Manager.

Take twelve fine, sound apricots; wipe carefully, cut them in two, remove the stones, and put them in a vessel with half a pound of powdered sugar, mashing them thoroughly. Then take two ounces of bitter almonds; peel and mash these while wet; add one gill of cold water and one ounce of powdered sugar, mashing the whole together. Place a muslin cloth over the vessel containing the mashed apricots and through it press the almond mixture. Stir all this together for four minutes; then add the juice of three lemons and a pint and a half of cold water. Beat thoroughly, then strain through a fine sieve into the freezer, and freeze as you do ice cream.

M. D. Owings

Pineapple Sherbet.

From Mrs. Governor Edwin C. Burleigh, of Maine, Second Vice-President Board of Lady Managers.

One quart grated pineapple, two heaping tablespoonfuls gelatine dissolved in hot water, one quart water, one quart sugar, juice of one large lemon, whites of two eggs well beaten put in just before freezing.

Mrs. Edwin C. Burleigh

Orange Water Ice.

From Mrs. Theo. F. Armstrong, of Delaware, Alternate Lady Manager.

Eight oranges, two lemons, the grated rind of two of the oranges boiled in a little water and then strained, two tablespoonfuls of corn starch mixed with a little cold water;

then pour boiling water on the starch; put in the juice of oranges and lemons after straining; one and one-half pounds sugar; add enough water to make one gallon, then freeze.

Mrs Theo F. Armstrong

Orange Frappée.

From Miss Annie M. Mahan, of West Virginia, Alternate Lady Manager.

One pint orange juice, one pint water, one pint sugar, juice of two lemons, grated rind of two oranges, partially freeze and pack in *ice only.*

Annie M. Mahan

BEVERAGES

Egg Nogg.

From Mrs. W. W. Kimball, of Chicago, Lady Manager.

One tablespoon of sugar; the yolk of one egg beaten with sugar; beat the white separately, stiff; add four spoons of brandy to beaten yolk; put half the white into mixture; half a glass of cream; then put the rest of the white on top.

Our Grandmother's Syllabub.

From Mrs. Sarah S. C. Angell of Michigan, Lady Manager.

One quart rich cream, juice and peel three lemons, one pint sherry wine, one quart pulverized sugar. Grate the lemon peels and express the juice, add sugar and pour over these the wine; stir until sugar is thoroughly moistened and then slowly add the cream. When mixed take whip-dash and with a tablespoon remove the floating bubbles which rise to the surface. Drop the contents of your spoon into lemonade or champagne glasses, continuing this process until all the cream is whipped. If the mixture becomes too thick and creamy to make bubbles, dilute it with sweet milk. This quantity will make thirty or forty glasses or fill a four-quart glass bowl. Great care must be taken not to dip the spoon too deeply into the mixture, the froth is what is desired.

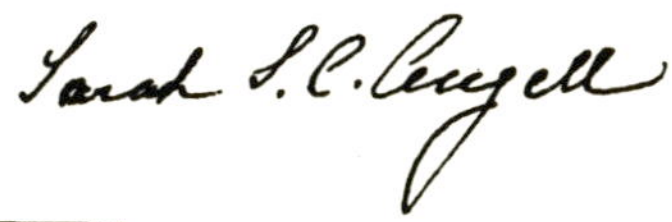

Claret Punch.

From Mrs. Frona Eunice Wait, of California, Alternate Lady Manager.

Take half a gallon of good claret and a pint of old whisky and mix them thoroughly; sweeten to taste by mixing the sugar with a little water to dissolve it before it comes in contact with the alcohol. Take a can of pineapple, or one fresh one, and chop fine, put juice and all into the punch; set the whole mixture on ice and let it stand at least three hours before using; serve some portion of the pineapple with each glass.

Beef Tea for Children.

From Mrs. Ida M. Ball, of Delaware, Lady Manager.

Use soup meat without bone cut into dice, and to every pound of meat use one pint of cold water. Cut up the meat on a dish, not on a board, as the latter absorbs the juices. Have the proper measure of water beside you in a soup basin or bowl, and as you cut up the meat sprinkle it moderately with salt and throw it into the cold water; there let it remain for two hours, then put it all into a sauce pan and set it on the fire. Watch carefully the first rising and skim and secure this as it is the very essence of the beef; put it into a clean bowl and let the beef go on boiling ten minutes, no longer; then pour the extract through a sieve to the first skimmings; stir before using. For older children than infants you may flavor with onion and a few cloves.

Ida M. Ball.

Chafing Dish

Lobster a la Newburg.

From Miss Mary Crease Sears, of Massachusetts, Alternate Lady Manager.

Two good-sized boiled lobsters. Pick out all the meat and cut into one-inch pieces. Place in a chafing dish with one ounce of butter, a pinch of salt and a very little red pepper. Cook five minutes, then add a wine glass of Madeira. Cook about three minutes, then add the yolks of three eggs well beaten with half a pint of sweet cream or milk; cook until it thickens, then serve.

Mary Crease Sears

Omelet.

From Mrs. Mary S. Lockwood, of District of Columbia, Lady Manager-at-Large.

Beat four fresh eggs slightly with two tablespoonfuls of cream; season with pepper and salt; put a tablespoonful of butter in the chafing dish, and when very hot pour in the egg; scrape up rapidly from all parts of the pan the cooked egg, letting the liquid portion follow the knife. It takes from forty to sixty seconds to cook it, then slip the knife under the left edge and fold the omelet over quickly and lightly. Serve on a hot dish.

Welsh Rarebit.

From MRS. COL. JAMES A. MULLIGAN, of Chicago, Lady Manager.

Take one pound of American cheese, cut up in small pieces, place in a chafing dish and season with half a salt-spoonful of red pepper; stir for ten minutes or until cheese is thoroughly melted; have ready six large pieces of toast on a very hot dish; cover each slice with the melted cheese; serve very hot as a relish.

Shrimp à la Newbnrg.

From MRS. HARRIET T. UPTON, of Ohio, Alternate Lady Manager.

One tablespoon butter; when hot add one tablespoon flour, four tablespoons cream stirred together; yolks of two eggs, add salt, red pepper and mace; bring to a scalding point, add shrimps and four tablespoons of sherry; serve at once.

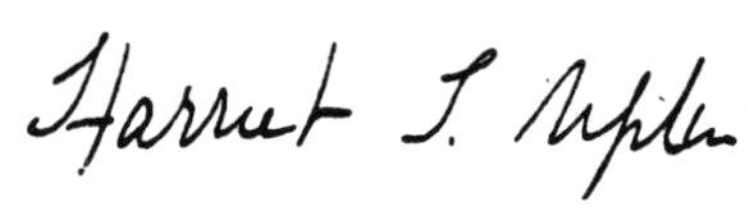

MRS. JAMES A. MULLIGAN.

Chicken with Currie.

From MRS. I. L. REQUA, of California, Alternate Lady Manager.

Mix half a teacupful of butter and two tablespoonfuls of currie powder thoroughly together, and put into the chafing dish with one small onion cut fine; stew together four minutes and then add half a teacupful of stock or broth, half teacupful milk, salt and pepper to taste; when this has become smooth add the chicken and stir constantly in the sauce, stewing nine minutes; serve with rice croquettes.

Fresh Mushrooms à la Crème.

From MRS. FRANCIS B. CLARKE, of Minnesota, Lady Manager.

Take a pound of fresh mushrooms, the larger the more tender; peel carefully the thin skin from the tops and wash thoroughly; then cut into broad strips or halves, if small, and place in a sauce pan with a pint of cream; let them boil slowly for a half to three-quarters of an hour, until tender; then take a little flour and a tablespoonful of butter, rub thoroughly together and mix into the cream; do not get it too thick; add salt and pepper and serve on hot toast. This also is very nice served in a chafing dish. Be sure to have the water in the under pan. Serve on toast. This makes a delicious luncheon dish.

Mock Terrapin.

From MRS. MARGARET BLAINE SALISBURY, of Utah, Eighth Vice-President Board of Lady Managers.

Put in the chafing dish the dark meat of cold chicken, turkey or grouse, cut in small dice, with half a pint of cream or stock, and when it comes to a boil stir in the following mixture: two tablespoons of butter rubbed into a smooth paste with a tablespoonful of flour and the yolks of three eggs, a teaspoonful dry mustard, a little cayenne pepper and salt, all mixed with a little cream or stock; let simmer a few minutes (not boil) and when ready to serve stir in a large wine-glass of Madeira.

Wishing you the success you deserve in the accomplishment of this laudable project, believe me,

Sincerely yours,

Margaret B. Salisbury